A Taste of

Kenyan Cooking

Other Kenway cookery books

Tastes of Kenya	Kathy Eldon & Eamon Mullan
Specialities of the House	Kathy Eldon
More Specialities of the House	Kathy Eldon
Mary Ominde's African Cookery of Kenya	Mary Ominde
Mpishi ya Kisasa	Terreza Zani
Karibu: Welcome to the cooking of Kenya	Anne Gardner
The modern African Vegetable Cookbook	Barbara Kimenye
The Kenya Cookery Book & Household Guide	St. Andrews Church Woman's Guild

A Taste of
Kenyan Cooking

Kenway Publications

Nairobi • Kampala • Dar es Salaam

Published in Kenya by
Kenway Publications
an imprint of
East African Educational Publishers Ltd.
Brick Court, Mpaka Road/Woodvale Grove
Westlands, P.O. Box 45314
Nairobi – 00100
KENYA.
Email: eaep@eastafricanpublishers.com
Website: www.eastafricanpublishers.com

East African Educational Publishers Ltd.
P.O. Box 11542
Kampala
UGANDA.

Ujuzi Books Ltd.
P.O. Box 38260,
Dar es Salaam
TANZANIA.

East African Publishers Rwanda Ltd.
No 86 Benjamina Street
Nyarutarama Gacuriro, Gasabo District
P.O. Box 5151, Kigali
RWANDA

First published in 1998
Reformatted and reprinted in 2010

ISBN 978-9966-46-610-5

Printed in Kenya by
Icons Printers Ltd.
P.O. Box 39273-00623
Nairobi, KENYA

Contents

Dedication

I dedicate this book to:
my mother, Mrs. A. M. Alam, for her love and patience;
my best friend and teacher Christian Caldara;
and last and sometimes least Auke Wiersma, for pulling faces whilst secretly
enjoying my cooking – often at the most ungodly hours.

Foreword

I welcome you to this Second Edition of *A Taste of Kenyan Cooking*, which I hope you will find interesting. The recipes are not only simple to follow but also very tasty. I have over 30 years experience of working in restaurants and clubs with fantastic chefs and managers. As you probably know Alan Bobbie was known practically the world over for his skills and wit. Christian Caldara follows closely with his unique style. Cooking is not only an art but also a science. When followed with dedication and love, amazing results are attained.

If you use good fresh products, you have already won half the battle. Have confidence and pride in your cooking and each dish you make will be savoured. I have revived some old classical dishes that were very popular years ago. They indeed have a place on our menus or platter if you try. I am tired of seeing this dribble of basalmic vinegar and towering food on our plates. Yes it's nice, but it's gone on too long ... let's get on with it. Presentation is important but then so is taste. One other thing taught to me to enhance your food: do mildly warm your plates before service – it will save you from having cold food.

Adil Karimbux
August 2010

Editor's note*

For many, cooking is something you learn in order to earn a living. For Adil Karimbux, cooking is a passion. From the age of six he was a constant presence in the kitchen of the family's Nakuru home, watching and helping Macharia, the cook, at his work. "What do you want to know about cooking for?" Macharia would chide. "This is a woman's profession."

"And why are you doing a woman's job, then?" came Adil's quick reply.

His interest reached a stage where his father, alarmed at this unusual trend, gave strict instructions that Adil should not be allowed in the kitchen any more. Undeterred, the young Adil took to spending Saturday afternoons with a friend from school, performing baking experiments that generally did not work too well, mostly because they would be over-generous with the baking powder.

As the household consisted of a grandmother, a great-aunt, two sisters and a mother, all of whom were almost always cooking, it was difficult for Adil to escape being influenced by the culinary processes he witnessed. Such was his curiosity that whenever the family was taken out for a meal, he would invariably find an opportunity to sneak into the restaurant kitchen to see how things were done.

And so Adil became the family joke, his sisters teasing him, "You don't even study; you'll end up being just a cook!"

Well, they were right – although "just" is hardly the word to describe the kind of cook Adil turned out to be. After school, trying his hand at computer programming, business administration, French and piloting (he has a pilot's licence), he ended up in the restaurant world learning the ropes more or less on the job. He has been a caterer at the Karen Country Club, worked at the Jardin de Paris, at the Café Frederique in the Netherlands, at Lavarini's Restaurant and at Alan Bobbe's Bistro where he has been a manager/partner for a number of years.

A Taste of Kenyan Cooking is Adil's first cookery collection. There are, of course, plenty of recipe books which expose the users to a wide variety of international cooking styles. However, there are few home-grown cookery books by local Kenyans in the cooking profession willing to share their skills and which, literally, bring haute cuisine home.

The present collection is aimed at you and I – people with an appreciation for food and the desire to experience it within the familiar environment of their own homes. The dishes described are commonly known and will appeal to the tastes of any household. What will most likely strike you about this book is the amazing ease with which you will be able to carry out, and eventually master, the preparation and cooking instructions. You will find that no particular dish is too difficult to prepare. All cooking processes described here can be done using utensils and other cooking implements that are available in most homes, and the author has taken the trouble to demystify most of the often intimidating processes used in advanced cookery. Even if you are on a tight budget, you will find that there are plenty of delicious recipes included here that will not cost very much to prepare, either for a special occasion or as a treat for the family.

I hope this book will do a lot to increase your confidence in your own culinary skills and to give you many happy hours in your kitchen. And for Adil, who could not wait for the book to be published, the next time his sisters ask for cooking tips he will not have to remind them about their "just a cook" joke; now, he is a cook with a book!

Joy W. N. Mutero
July 1998

*Note to the first Edition

How to use this book

Wherever a recipe indicates the need for using stock, please try to use fresh stock as far as possible, in spite of the fact that some of the recipes quote stock cubes. Shop-bought cubes are usually very salty and for this reason one should try to avoid them. Similarly, it is preferable to use fresh garlic and ginger as the powdered variety does not give the desired result. For salads, Italian, French and Spanish recipes, use extra virgin olive oil for the best results.

Before trying out the recipes in this collection, study the glossary at the end for more useful details. The weights and measures are approximate, as every cook has his or her preferences as to how they prefer to blend the various ingredients. Avoid interchanging metric and imperial measures. They do not mix. When serving hot meals, warm your plates; you won't believe how much of a difference this makes.

All the recipes are given in good faith. Any errors that may have occurred during publishing are not the responsibility of the author or of the publisher.

Chapter 1

Soups

Courgette (zucchini) soup with a hint of mint

A velvety soup of distinction, an emblem of the season and above all leaves you with a lot of time to attend to other chores as it can be prepared well in advance. Enjoy!

Ingredients

- enough good olive oil to cover a large pan comfortably, with a 2cm slab of butte thrown in
- 2 onions grated
- 10 medium courgettes grated
- 4 cloves garlic crushed
- 5 stock cubes (of your choice, not fish)
- 2 bunches chopped mint
- 2 cups milk
- 6 tsp corn flour mixed with a cup of water... do this just before using as otherwise the corn flour 'sets'
- ½ cup double cream
- salt and pepper to taste
- 1 cup grater parmesan or strong cheddar cheese to sprinkle at the end
- croutons (to be floated on the soup just before serving)

Method

Croutons

- Pre-heat oven to 190°C.
- 8 slices of bread, crust cut of, cubed to bite size and coated generously with good olive oil, placed on a tray in the oven for 10-15 minutes or till nicely golden.
- Try to do the croutons just before serving.
- It does not take much time and the result will pay off.
- Can add garlic if so desired.

The soup

- Heat the olive oil/butter mix on a medium flame. Fry the onions till soft, add the courgettes, stir fry for about 5 minutes then add the garlic.

- Sauté this for another 5 minutes, add the stock cubes, mint, milk and corn flour mix.
- The soup should start to thicken, add the cream, do not boil, check seasoning and correct if need be.
- Before serving, warm your soup plates, ladle it out, sprinkle the cheese and float the crisp croutons and run to the table.

Serves 8   ·

Brown bean soup

This recipe comes from the Netherlands and I learned it from a lady in Friesland. It is actually a rival to their pea soup. Bean soup is normally eaten with bread and is more than adequate as a complete meal.

Ingredients

- 1 kg (2.2 lb) brown beans cleaned and soaked for at least 4 hours.
- 1 potato, cubed
- 1 bunch parsley, chopped
- 2 leeks, washed and sliced
- 2 onions, chopped
- 3 bunches celery stalks, chopped
- 3 stock cubes
- 3 tbsp butter
- 1 l (35 fl oz) water
- ½ l (17.5 fl oz) milk
- 8 slices smoked cooked beef, chopped (optional) or ham
- salt and pepper to taste

Method

- Boil the beans in water for half an hour.
- Melt the butter and add the onions, leeks and celery.
- Sauté until soft, add water and return the beans to the pot with the potatoes, parsley and stock cubes.
- Bring to the boil and simmer for at least 2 hours, making sure the water does not dry out. When all the ingredients are tender, put the mixture through a blender or a sieve, trying not to leave too much of a residue.
- Return to the pan and simmer, adding milk as desired. (Normally this soup is very thick).
- Add the smoked beef. Season.

Serves 6

Traditional split pea soup

Ingredients

- 8 l hot water
- 2½ cups split peas, soaked overnight
- 4 leeks, chopped
- 2 celery sticks, sliced
- ½ l (18 oz) cream and ½ tsp corn flour, blended together
- 4 onions, finely chopped
- 1 carrot, chopped
- 3 potatoes, peeled
- 1 kg (2.2 lb) veal bones
- 1 kg (2.2 lb) knuckle of lamb!
- 10 slices beef bacon, chopped and cooked (optional)
- 4 tbsp vegetable oil
- salt and pepper
- a little sugar
- parsley, chopped, to garnish

Method

- Place the vegetables, bones and meat in a large pan with the oil and sauté over a low to medium flame.
- Add hot water and split peas, cover and cook for at least 4¼ hours at medium heat, checking the water constantly. Add more if necessary.
- Remove the meat and bones. Scrape the meat off the bones and return it to the pot. Lower the heat. Add the cream and corn flour and season.
- You may like to add the beef bacon. Garnish and stir.
- This soup should be quite thick.

Hint: Sometimes the quality of split peas is poor. Ideally they should have a pale green colour, not yellow. Usualy a pork trotter is added. This increases the cooking time by ar least 2 hours.

Serves 6

. . . .

Chilled cucumber soup

Ingredients

- 2 medium cucumbers, thinly sliced and blanched
- 2 medium onions, thinly sliced
- 2 tbsp butter
- 2 stock cubes dissolved in 600 ml (1 pint) warm water
- 3 tsp lime juice
- 2 tsp corn flour blended with a little water
- ½ cup cream
- a pinch of paprika powder
- salt and pepper to taste
- mint leaves to garnish

Method

- Sauté the onion and cucumber in butter, then add the water and stock cubes.
- Simmer for 10 minutes. Sieve finely.
- Add seasoning, lemon juice and corn flour.
- Continue to simmer for 5 minutes. Chill, stir in half cup cream.
- Sprinkle a little paprika and mint leaves on top.

Serves 4

. . . .

Mixed lentil soup

This soup is not usually very popular. However, in this recipe the different types of lentils cooked together have a pleasant taste and bring out the best in the cook too!

Ingredients

- 3 cups mixed lentils (yellow split, red split and chana)
- 2 tsp butter or oil
- 2 medium onions
- 2 tomatoes, skinned and sliced
- 2 tbsp lemon juice
- 4 slices of smoked beef (optional)
- 2 stock cubes
- 4 cloves garlic, crushed
- 1 tsp ginger, crushed
- 9 cups (2 l) water
- salt and pepper to taste

Method

- Make sure the lentils are clean. If possible, soak for a few hours.
- Run them through cold water until clear.
- Boil lentils for about 5 minutes alone in about 2 l water.
- Skim off the froth and drain the water.
- Return the lentils to the pan with the oil or butter.
- Add onions, tomatoes, garlic and ginger and fry this over a medium flame for about 10 minutes, stirring all the time.
- Add the water and stock cubes, then simmer for about an hour.
- When cooked, whisk carefully to break up any whole lentils.
- Add a little water to achieve the desired consistency.
- Add lemon juice, salt and pepper to taste, and smoked beef. Serve hot.

Serves 6

. . . .

Tomato soup

An old favourite that never fails to satisfy.

Ingredients

- 1 kg (2.2 lb) tomatoes (with skin), sliced
- 2 potatoes, peeled and diced
- 3 onions, finely chopped
- 4 cloves garlic, crushed
- 4 tbsp butter
- 2 tbsp oil
- 2 stock cubes, crushed
- 750 ml (1.2 pints) water
- 2 tbsp red wine
- 5 tbsp cream or juice of 2 oranges
- 2 bay leaves
- ¼ tbsp mixed herbs
- paprika according to your taste
- sugar according to your taste
- salt and pepper to taste
- 1 tbsp tomato puree to thicken (optional)
- parsley
- basil

Method

- In a large pan, fry the onions in the butter and oil for a few minutes.
- Add the tomatoes and garlic and let them cook for 4 minutes over medium heat.
- Add the water, crushed stock cubes, wine, potatoes, mixed herbs and bay leaves.

Leave to simmer for 20 minutes.

- Remove the pan from the fire and drain everything through a colander or sieve, preserving the liquid.
- Puree using a sieve or blender. (If sieved, discard what remains in the sieve).
- Return the liquid and blended ingredients to the pot and simmer again, adding seasoning, paprika and sugar according to your taste.
- Add tomato puree if a thicker consistency is desired.
- Do not let the soup boil. Stir in the orange juice or cream and garnish with parsley and basil.

Serves 4

. . . .

Chicken soup with couscous

Chunky and wholesome

Ingredients

- 1 chicken, cut up (a "road-runner" is best)
- ½ cup cous-cous
- 2 turnips, diced and peeled
- 2 tbsp butter
- 3 onions
- 3 cloves garlic, chopped
- 2 medium-sized sticks cinnamon
- 1 clove
- 1 chicken stock cube dissolved in 1 l warm water
- milk
- salt and pepper

Method

- Brown the chicken in a pan with the butter and onions.
- Add the stock, cinnamon, clove and garlic.
- Simmer for at least 2 hours if it is a tough old 'road-runner' or for 40 minutes if you're using a "softie." Then take the chicken off the pan and remove the meat from the bone using a strong fork and knife.
- Return the meat to the pan and let it continue to simmer for a few minutes.
- Season and add the turnips, milk and couscous (this normally cooks in 20 minutes unless otherwise stated by the manufacturers).

Serves 4

. . . .

Chilled avocado soup

As the name suggests, serve very cold.

Ingredients

- 3 medium ripe avocados
- 1 onion, finely chopped and lightly fried in 1 tbsp butter
- 1 bunch spring onions, finely chopped
- juice of 2 limes
- 160 ml (6 oz) cream, lightly whipped
- a dash of worcestershire sauce
- a dash of tabasco
- 2 stock cubes dissolved in 600 ml hot water and cooled
- salt and pepper to taste

Method

- Skin the avocados, remove the seed and puree using either a nylon sieve or a liquidizer.
- Add the fried onion and continue liquidizing while slowly adding the stock. When all the stock is mixed, add the lime juice, seasoning, tabasco and worcestershire sauce.
- Pour into a large bowl, chill well, check seasoning and serve sprinkled with the chopped spring onions and cream.
- You may also want to add a little finely chopped dhania (cilantro).

Serves 4

· ·

Beetroot borscht

A cold Polish/Euro soup that is refreshing and wonderful especially on hot days, chill well and top with sour cream just before serving (you may use double cream instead). In a pot, boil together till tender:

Ingredients

- 4 potatoes
- 1 parsnip

- When cooked dice and keep aside. Now boil the beetroots untill done – approximately 1 hour (with skin). 1 ½ kg beetroot.
- When done, peel and dice half very finely and liquidize the other half (add a cup of water to help). Keep aside.

Ingredients

- 1 tbsp olive oil
- 2 onions chopped
- 3 celery sticks chopped
- 3 carrots diced
- 3 cloves of garlic crushed
- 3 cups beef or chicken stock (2 stock cubes in hot water)
- juice of 1 lime
- ¼ cup wine vinegar
- 2 tsp sugar
- salt and freshly milled pepper
- 5 tbsp sour cream
- 4 tbsp fresh dill, chopped

Method

- In a pan sauté the onions with the oil, add the celery and carrots, brown slightly.
- Add garlic, then the stock half a minute later and lime juice, wine vinegar, sugar followed by the diced potatoes, parsnip and beetroot (diced and liquidized).
- Checkthe seasoning and correct. Chill. Place your soup plates in the freezer. When ready dish out and top with the sour cream and fresh dill. Sometimes it is better to check the seasoning again. When it is really cold, it changes again.

Serves 4

Chapter 2

Breakfast, Salads and Starters

Chilli paneer

A wonderful dish for vegetarians, though even carnivores take to it. I wonder why this is so expensive when we eat out given how affordable the whole thing is. Is it inflation or greed?

Ingredients

- 1 block paneer cubed
- 2 tsp lime juice
- 1 tsp flour (plain)
- 1 tsp corn flour
- ½ tsp salt

Method

- Mix the above and set aside.

For the rest, combine in a pan:

Ingredients

- 4 tbsp oil
- 4 green chillies split in ½
- 1 tbsp ginger crushed
- 1 tbsp garlic crushed
- ½ tsp salt and ½ tsp pepper
- 1 tsp cumin seeds
- 1 tsp tomato puree
- ½ tsp sugar
- ½ tsp red chilli powder
- 1 tsp vinegar (white wine or malt)
- chopped spring onions and fresh dhania to add at the end

Method

- Sauté these over a high flame, for about 5 minutes. If the mix gets too dry, add some water.
- Mix in the paneer and heat through. Check the seasoning and adjust. Top with the spring onions and dhania.

Spinach and vegetable fritters

Normally eaten as a snack with ice cold beer and a delightful dipping sauce.

Ingredients

- dipping sauce
  Place in a liquidizer
- 2 bunches of fresh coriander leaves
- 1 cup of very thick yoghurt (you may add a little more if needed)
- 4 green chillies (add or subtract according to taste
- 1 level tsp freshly ground ginger
- salt and pepper

Method

- Whizz this to a fine sauce, remove and put into a bowl, add a little more yoghurt to thicken.
- Season well with salt and pepper.
- Keep in the refrigerator and use when required.

The batter

Ingredients

- 2½ cups gram flour shifted
- ¾ cup water
- ¼ cup yoghurt
- 2 tsp cumin seeds
- 1 tsp coriander powder
- ½ bunch fresh coriander leaves, chopped finely
- ¼ tsp carom seeds (also known as bishops weed or ajwain – available from Indian spice shops, pick for stones)
- 1 level spoon salt

Method

- In a bowl, mix this well adding the liquid gradually, breaking any lumps that form.
- Keep aside.

The vegetables

Ingredients

- 2 potatoes peeled and cut into fine cubes
- 1 small bunch sukuma finely chopped
- 1 small carrot cubed
- 1 zucchini cubed

- Add these vegetables to your batter. You may use your favourite vegetables instead like aubergine, cabbages or onions. Plain onion rings are delicious too.

To fry

- In what we call a *karahi* or deep wok, add enough oil to deep fry.
- Keep the heat medium to high.
- Drop the battered vegetables in small amounts and deep fry till golden brown.
- Test one first to make sure it is cooked.
- Serve with the dipping sauce. Great with sundowners and cocktails.

Serves 4

....

Beetroot raita

A stunning tasty and cooling salad.

Ingredients

- 10 medium beets, washed, trimmed and placed in an oven at 200°C for 1 hour or till soft. Cooled then peeled and cubed.
- set aside.
- 2 onions chopped finely
- 1 carton thick Indian or Greek yoghurt
- salt, pepper, and a good pinch chilli added according to taste.

Method

- Mix the ingredients together and season well. Chill in the refrigerator. Serve with fiery hot curries, soothing roasts, or a simple lettuce, cucumber and spinach salad.

Serves 4

....

Spinach salad with strawberries and brie

Refreshing, cool, light also a main course and dessert in one dish.

Ingredients

- 1 punnet strawberries, washed and sliced
- 2 packs Italian spinach washed and dried in salad spinner (about 3 bunches)
- 1 disc brie (kept cold and cut into cubes)
- ¼ cup poppy seeds
- ½ cup sesame seeds slightly toasted
- 1 cup virgin olive oil

- ½ cup raspberry vinegar (or wine vinegar with a good handful of fresh raspberries, crushed, added and shaken well as a substitute)
- 1 cup sugar
- 1 tbsp finely chopped onion
- good dash of leas and Perrins
- salt, pepper, paprika to taste

Method

- Combine the sugar and vinegar till dissolved, add the oil, whisking well followed by all the rest of the ingredients except the spinach, strawberries and brie.
- Taste the seasoning and adjust accordingly.
- Arrange the spinach, strawberries and brie on a large platter and before serving add the dressing. Ideally the dressing should be chilled.
- Cool, smooth and quite delicious.

Serves 2

. . . .

Nairobi chicken wings

A starter or a snack with drinks. Either way, this is something that you will love as you drown a cool beer...

Ingredients

- 1 kilo chicken wings
- 1 tbsp garlic and ginger
- 2 tbsp oil
- 1 tbsp salt
- 1 tbsp corn flour diluted in a little water
- 1 tbsp tabasco or green chillie minced according to taste
- 4 tbsp light soya sauce
- 2 tbsp lime juice
- 2 tbsp honey
- salt and pepper to taste
- lightly toasted sesame seeds and spring onions to garnish

Method

- Wash and dry the chicken wings.
- Blitz the other ingredients in a liquidizer (not the wings).
- Marinate in the refrigerator for at least 4 hours or overnight.
- Remove ½ an hour before using.

- Put your grill on nearly full and grill for about 10 minutes, basting with a little extra oil.
- Serve immediately.
- Sprinkle the sesame seeds and spring onions.

Serves 4

. . . .

Bean soup with basil

A hearty soup, quick to make and once again do add ingredients that are just hanging around your refrigerator.

Ingredients

- ½ cup olive oil
- 2 onions finely chopped
- 3 celery sticks chopped (cleaned)
- 1 leek sliced (cleaned)
- 3 carrots diced
- 4 cups chicken stock (2 stock cubes in 4 cups hot water)
- 1½ cup white wine
- 1½ tsp sugar
- 2 cans of beans drained and rinsed (use cannellini, kidney or butter. They are extremely (affordable) salt and pepper

Add at the very end – minutes before serving

- 4 cloves garlic crushed
- ½ cup chopped basil
- ½ cup chopped parsley

Method

- In a large pan, heat the oil and add the onions. Saute till soft.
- Add the celery, leek and carrot and continue to fry for a few minutes.
- Add the stock, wine and sugar.
- Bring to the boil, reduce heat and simmer for 20 minutes, then add the beans.
- Using a potato masher, mash the beans and vegetables a bit (not puree, leave some whole!).
- Check the seasoning, stir in the garlic, basil and parsley, heat through and serve on warmed plates.

Serves 4 – 6

. . . .

Chilled avocado soup – a slant on the original

Kenya has the most wonderful creamy avocados, at the most reasonable prices. I have modified this recipe to suit our tastes here and think that it reflects this. It's healthy, fulfilling and magically wonderful...

Ingredients

- 4 medium ripe avocados, peeled and seeded
- 2 stock cubes – chicken or vegetable – dissolved in 600 ml hot water and cooled
- juice of two limes
- a dash Worcestershire sauce
- a double dash Tabasco
- 2 onions very finely chopped, and 2 cloves garlic crushed and fried in a tbsp of olive oil for 2 minutes
- 160 ml double cream
- 1 can crab, drained, or a handful of cooked prawns (shrimp)
- salt and pepper to taste
- 20 cubes of bread 2 cm by 2 cm lightly coated in olive oil and placed in an oven at 200°C till lightly browned (now they are crutons!)
- ½ bunch spring onions and ½ bunch chives chopped fine

Method

- Place the avocado in a blender with the cooled stock. Place lid firmly on, everytime you use it as it tends to jump at your face.
- Whizz till smooth, add the lime juice, Worcestershire sauce and tabasco.
- Give it a couple more whizzes and place in a bowl, adding the onion, garlic mix, the double cream and the crab or prawns.
- Fold in, season well with the salt and pepper.
- Chill really well.
- Place the soup plates in the freezer if you can. When ready serve the soup on the cooled plates. Taste as it will change as it cools, adjust seasoning.
- Place the crutons on the soup, sprinkle with the spring onions and chives. If you are vegetarian, simply use the vegetable stock. Omit the crab or shrimp.
- Peel a large cucumber, de-seed it, cut into small segments and add tsp of salt and place in a sieve for half an hour.
- Drain, rinse and add to your soup. A delicate soup, consoling on a hot summers day and so very good for you.

Serves 4

Dal (lentil) soup – ndengu

I have modified this to a soup recipe. You can have it with rice, and for sure it will be a comforting meal and so affordable. You can also add bits of leftover meat, shredded (at the end). It may look difficult but if all the ingredients are lined up. It will be ever so easy.

Ingredients

- 2 cups of yellow dal (or dal of your choice – even mixed dal is good) soaked in water, for about 4 hours, then drained and rinsed. Place in a pan with the following:
- 12 cups of water
- 1 chicken stock cube
- 6 tomatoes chopped
- 4 onions thinly sliced
- 10 cloves of garlic crushed
- 1 tbsp fresh ginger pounded
- 1 tsp turmeric
- 3 sticks of cinnamon
- 6 cloves

Method

- Let the lentils boil, then simmer for about 2½ hours, stirring every now and then, also skimming. Then add:
  - 3 tbsp lemon juice
  - 2 tsp salt
  - 2 tsp sugar (optional)
  - black pepper, red chilli powder according to taste
- Mix well, now 'temper the dal' (place about 5 tbsp oil in a small pan almost to smoking point and quickly add:
  - 2 tbsp whole mustard seeds
  - 2 tbsp whole cumin
  - 1 tbsp coriander powder
  - a good pinch asafoetida (optional)
  - 10 fresh curry leaves
- The mustard seeds will pop and you will smell the spices almost immediately. Pour this over the dal carefully and it will sizzle. Stir and add:
  - some powdered fenugreek (optional)
  - a bunch of fresh coriander chopped
  - Some green chillies
- Check the seasoning – you may need more salt, chilli, lemon or sugar according to your taste.

- Bring to boil and serve. If you have difficulties obtaining some of these spices, go to any Indian ration store. Here in Nairobi most of them are situated in the mighty Highridge area. Fenugreek is known as *methi,* and asafetida is known as *hing.*
- *Hing* smells awful when raw, but tempered, it changes and is reputed to calm your stomach. Have a go at this and later experiment with other dals (lentils).

Serves 4 – 6

. . . .

Mom's noodle soup

An economical soup as you may just about add all the leftover vegetables in your fridge, be it spinach or carrots. You may add cold cuts of meat, beef, chicken or shrimp from your freezer.

Ingredients

- 4 cups chicken stock (if using cubes use 2 first and see if you like it. Stock cubes vary a lot so it is better to put less and add later
  - 3 tbsp soya sauce
  - 2 tsp sesame oil
  - 2 tsp sugar
  - 1 chopped green chilli
  - 2 cloves garlic crushed
  - 2 tsp grated ginger
  - 2 tbsp dry sherry
  - 200 gm noodles of your choice (fine ones are better)
  - chopped coriander (dhania) to sprinkle on at the end

Method

- Add cooked beef, chicken, or vegetables of your choice like finely chopped
- spinach, carrots, mushrooms, corn etc. If using shrimp, add the last few minutes as it cooks very quickly.
- In a large pot, over a medium heat add all the ingredients except for the noodlesand shrimp, if using.
- Bring to boil, add the noodles, cook till done (6 minutes usually) then add the shrimp.
- Check the seasoning. It is also nice to add chicken, beef and shrimp. Try out variations.

Serves 4

. . . .

Tomato soup – again a variation

Very warming and comforting. Add the garlic and basil minutes before serving.

Ingredients

- ½ cup olive oil
- 3 onions finely chopped
- 3 carrots diced very finely
- 800 ml hot water
- 2 chicken stock cubes
- 2 cans good tomatoes, diced and juice retained
- juice of two fresh oranges
- 4 tbsp tomato puree (may need more)
- 1 tsp grated ginger
- 2 tsp sugar
- salt and freshly milled pepper
- 7 cloves garlic crushed
- 15 basil leaves torn
- parsley to sprinkle at the end

Method

- In a large pan over a medium heat, sauté the onions till clear, add the carrots and fry for another 3 minutes,
- Add the hot water and the stock, stir well and then add all the ingredients except for the garlic and basil.
- Just before serving, heat through and add the garlic and the basil, heat for about 4 minutes, check the seasoning and correct if needed.
- Serve with good French bread, sliced and coated with your favourite cheese.
- Heat your soup plates in the oven and it will really be piping hot. Kids love it too.

Serves 4

. . . .

Chickpea gazpacho

A rich cooling soup, serve chilled with lots of crusty bread.

Ingredients

- 1 can chickpeas, drained and rinsed
- 1 can good canned tomatoes, chopped
- 1½ cup tomato juice
- 1 cup chicken stock (use stock cubes – about one)
- 1 punnet cherry tomatoes (if not available use small regular ones)

- 1 cucumber peeled seeded and diced
- 2 small onions finely chopped
- ½ bunch fresh coriander (dhania) chopped
- 4 tbsp lime juice
- 1 tsp fresh ginger grated
- 2 cloves garlic crushed
- ½ spoon salt
- ½ spoon pepper
- good dash of lea and perrins (it's the best one)
- good dash Tabasco
- extra fresh coriander to sprinkle on before serving

Method
- Mix in all the ingredients, check seasoning, and chill. If your refrigerator has a large freezer compartment, put in your soup bowls.
- Serve when you are ready. This gives you the added advantage to attend to other chores.

Serves 4

....

Limuru spicy chicken wings

Full of flavour and a starter that will be remembered for days.

Ingredients

Marinate together overnight:
- 1 kg chicken wings (plump ones!)
- ½ cup lime juice
- 1 tsp salt
- ½ tsp red chilli

Next day drain excess liquid and add:
- 1½ tsp ginger
- 1½ tsp garlic
- 1 large onion grated
- 2 tbsp oil
- 1 tbsp corn flour
- 2 tbsp soy sauce
- 2 tbsp honey or brown sugar
- good dash tabasco

Method

- Let this marinate now for 4 hours. Then grill under full heat for about 9 minutes or till done.
- Check seasoning (especially salt).
- Serve piping hot with lots of napkins and bowls for the bones.

Serves 4

· · · · · · · · · · · · · · · · · · · ·

Kenyan baked asparagus

A neat recipe that can be prepared earlier and simply popped in the oven to finish off. A wonderful starter.

Ingredients

- ½ kg asparagus, washed and held about half way with both hands, using two fingers and bent.
  The asparagus should break at approximately the correct place
- 2 tbsp butter
- 1 tomato seeded and chopped
- salt and freshly milled pepper
- a little lemon juice
- ½ cup parmesan mixed with about the same cubed buffalo mozzarella

Method

- In a pan bring some salted water to boil.
- Drop the asparagus in and blanch for about 4 minutes.
- Remove and rinse under cold water.
- Grease a baking tray and place the asparagus in it.
- Dot with butter, tomato, seasoning and lemon juice.
- Pre-heat the oven to 200°C and bake for 12 minutes.
- Remove and dot with cheese, replace in oven and let it bake for another 5 minutes or till tender. You could also sprinkle some crispy bacon on before serving if you like.

Serves 4

· · · · · · · · · · · · · · · · · · · ·

Stir fried calamari

Usually people are intimidated by Calamari. Ask your fishmonger to teach you how to clean it. It is pretty simple. Remove the transparent sharp bone, rinse in salted water and cut into rings, dry it with some tissue and finely dust with baking flour.

Ingredients

- ½ kg calamari
- 2 cups home baking flour
- 2 tsp paprika
- 1 tsp chilli
- ½ tsp salt
- ½ tsp freshly milled pepper

Method

- Heat in a large pan a ¼ cup olive oil, heated slowly with 3 cloves garlic, remove garlic as it just begins to brown a little.
- Increase heat and drop the calamari in the oil (in batches and increase oil if needed).
- Sauté for only 2 minutes. Keep warm as you finish cooking the rest. Serve with some mayonnaise flavoured with additional garlic if you please and a large green salad.

Serves 2

. . . .

Shrimp in a garlic sauce

Ideal to go with your sundowners, really quick to prepare and ever so tasty.

Ingredients

- medium size shrimp, shelled and deveined
- ½ tsp salt
- 4 tbsp olive oil
- 5 cloves garlic crushed
- ½ spoon paprika (smoked is even better)
- ½ spoon chilli pepper (more or less as you like)
- ½ spoon freshly milled pepper
- few drops lime juice
- some chopped parsley to garnish

Method

- Let the shrimp sit in a bowl of water (not too much) with the salt, for 20 minutes
- This seasons the shrimp and gets rid of the fishy smell.
- Discard the water and pat the shrimp dry without rinsing.
- Heat the oil, add the garlic, paprika, chilli, lime juice and finally the shrimp. "Stir-fry" for about 3 minutes (the shrimp will turn pink).
- Sprinkle with parsley, taste one to check the seasoning and do correct it if need be.
- Place on a warmed platter and with toothpicks and napkins, run to your guests and enjoy.

Serves 4

. . . .

Great guacamole

There is guacamole and guacamole, this one is in its own right gorgeous. Use your favourite Kenyan chips, papadums or tacos to dip in and enjoy. If you like it creamy smooth like I do, place in a food processor; if its chunky you are after, then use a fork and manual labour.

Ingredients

Into a food processor add:
- 4 avocados (skin and pits removed)
- 6 tbsp double cream
- 1 tsp ground cumin
- ½ tsp oregano
- 2 cloves garlic chopped
- 1 onion halved
- 1 bunch coriander (dhania), or less if you prefer
- 3 tbsp lime juice
- 1 tsp salt
- good shake of Tabasco or cayenne pepper to taste

Method

- Whizz this and put into a bowl and refrigerate.
- If on diet, use celery sticks or carrots to dip into. Either way it is yummy.

Serves 4

. . . .

Marinated goats cheese (or olives)

A nice way of adding your own touch to cheese or olives. Remember to let the product marinate for at least 4 days. Check the 'best by' dates to be safe.

Ingredients

- one jar, large enough to accommodate the cheese disc or olives
- 3 – 4 discs goat cheese or the equivalent of olives
- 4 peeled cloves garlic
- 6 – 8 whole pepper corns
- some tarragon
- some thyme (equivalent of 1 tbsp)
- 1 tsp salt
- olive oil to cover

Method

- Put all the ingredients together in a jar and cover with the olive oil.
- Seal and shake the jar delicately.
- Refrigerate and use after 4 days.
- Shake it from time to time.

Serves 6

....

Chicken peanut and coconut soup

A rich soup, full of character and simply the best, combination of East African cultures.

Ingredients

- 2 cups peanuts, skins removed, roasted and finely ground in a food processor (keep aside for now)
- ¼ cup oil
- 2 large onions finely chopped
- 4 large tomatoes, finely chopped
- 1 tsp cumin
- 4 cloves garlic crushed
- 2 tsp ginger
- 1 plump chicken, halved (we have to debone it once cooked)
- 4 cups hot water with a stock cube of your choice dissolved in it
- 2 cups thick coconut milk
- 1 bunch very finely chopped dhania (coriander), a good dash lemon, salt, pepper and red chilli, all to be added at the very end, having taken the soup off the boil

Method

- In a large pan on a medium heat, sauté the onions till a little brown.
- Add the tomatoes, cook till soft, sprinkle the cumin followed by the garlic and ginger, stir well.
- Add the chicken, the stock, and coconut milk, reduce heat to a simmer.
- Sprinkle the ground peanuts into this.
- Let this cook on a low heat for about 25 minutes or till the chicken is just tender.
- Remove the chicken, let cool a little and separate the bones.
- Cut the chicken flesh into bite size bits, and return the meat to the pan.
- Season with salt pepper, chilli, lemon and dhania and stir well to taste.
- This is the time to have the seasoning absolutely correct.
- Serve and watch each face light up as this fine soup hits the spot!

Serves 4

. . . .

Avocado mousse

Like most vegetables and fruit in Kenya, the avocado here is quite remarkable in flavour, texture and size … my favourite recipe often for grand occasions.

Ingredients

- 2 large avocados, peeled, seed removed and pureed in a food processor (till smooth) or use a plastic sieve
- add the juice of one lime (or according to taste)
- 225 gm cream cheese
- 4 cloves garlic crushed
- 2 tbsp spring onions chopped
- 1 cucumber deseeded, cubed, placed in a sieve with one tsp salt, over a bowl to get rid of the excess water. After 20 minutes rinse well with water and pat dry with kitchen paper or clean cloth
- dash lea and perrins
- I tbsp extra virgin olive oil
- dash tabasco
- salt and pepper to taste
- some flaked almonds or cashews to decorate and chopped parsley
- 1 plump chicken, halved (we have to debone it once cooked)

Method

- Gradually add the rest of the ingredients to the avocado (the lemon should go in almost as you puree the avocado to prevent it going brown).
- Place in a bowl, check the seasoning, and correct it if need be.
- Sprinkle the flaked nuts and the chopped parsley on top, chill well.
- Serve with warmed baguette, wholemeal toasts, etc.

Serves 4

. . . .

Yummy artichoke dips

A delicious, hot dip and a sure winner at parties. Serve with local crisps, tortilla chips, (warmed through briefly in the oven) or even papadums. I think it is fabulous and hope you do too.

Ingredients

- 1 can artichoke hearts, drained and roughly chopped
- 300 ml mayonnaise
- 150 gm parmesan cheese grated
- 75 gm mozzarella grated (put in the freezer for 10 minutes and then grate)
- 2 green chillies finely chopped
- a handful of chopped fresh coriander (optional)
- salt and pepper to taste
- good handful chopped almonds, or pistachios (even cashews if you wish)

Method

- Pre-heat the oven to 200°C. Mix all the ingredients above together, check seasoning and correct, placing in a baking tin no more than 2 cm deep.
- Sprinkle the nuts on top and dust with paprika or some red chilli for colour.
- Bake for about 18 minutes, till bubbly and slightly golden.
- Serve hot, with thin warmed buttery pitta bread or crusty bread. This will seal your destiny as queen of the kitchen.

Serves 6

Black olive paté

A tasty Paté that suits vegetarians. Serve with warm French bread.

Ingredients

- 230 gm pitted black olives
- juice and rind of ½ lemon (try to get organic otherwise omit the rind... which is a pity, but better not to get poisoned slowly)
- 1½ tbsp extra virgin olive oil
- 25 gm fresh breadcrumbs (use the large holes in a grater to do this. Any larger chunks that escape should not be used. This bit can be fiddly but try to persevere)
- 60 gm soft unsalted butter
- a pinch salt and a good mill of pepper

Method

- Place the olives in a food processor and whizz. If you find that they do not break up easily, add a little olive oil to assist this.
- Remove and place in a bowl, add the rest of the ingredients mix well and chill for at least four hours.
- Serve with warm French bread.

Serves 4 – 6

....

Waldorf salad

A classic salad, not spotted on the menu these days, but has a place in history and on our plates. It's fresh, cool, and very tasty.

Ingredients

- 3 large crisp apples halved, cored and diced. Coated with a little lemon juice to prevent browning
- 4 celery sticks, washed and thinly sliced
- 1 cup walnuts chopped (pecans can be permitted)
- ½ cup chopped dates or figs (optional)
- 1 cup mayonnaise
- season with salt and pepper
- some lettuce, tomatoes or cucumber to decorate the plated or platter

Method

- In a bowl combine all the ingredients except the ones for décor.
- Chill nicely in the refrigerator and when ready to eat place on plates, arranged with the extra garnish.
- Another forgotten salad that needs to come back and grace our plates.

Serves 2

. . . .

Cool Lamu shrimp salad

Do not hesitate to add your own ingredients like avocados, cherry tomatoes or cucumbers. You may stumble on something that is a great hit.

Ingredients

- 1 kg small shrimp, shelled, deveined and cooked. (Boil some water with some salt and a dash lemon juice, add the shrimp, they will turn pink pretty soon. When this happens they are done. Rinse immediately under cold running water. Try not to overcook as they turn into pellets)
- 1 celery stalk, washed then diced thinly
- 2 small carrots washed and thinly sliced
- 1 tbsp sweet pickle relish (or chop up some gherkins and sweeten lightly with sugar as a subtitute)
- ½ a cup mayonnaise
- 2 tsp low fat sour cream
- 3 tbsp tomato ketchup
- ½ lime juice
- 3 tsp chopped dill
- a dash of tabasco, salt and pepper to taste
- some fresh crisp lettuce or very thinly sliced, blanched cabbage to lay on the platter before serving

Method

- Combine all the ingredients except for the lettuce/cabbage.
- Taste for seasoning, cool in the refrigerator and serve on a large platter arranged with the lettuce, and or cabbage.
- To enhance appearance, dust with paprika or chilli.

Serves 4

. . . .

American shrimp (prawn cocktail)

Whilst in the USA I was once asked to cook a shrimp cocktail for a family. To my delight it was an easy fate ... ketchup, mayonnaise, lemon juice, lea and perrins, dash Tabasco, salt and pepper. I did not realize that the American cocktail is entirely different and equally as delicious. My friends were not amused with my cocktail...alas!

Ingredients

- ½ kg cooked prawns shelled and deveined (to cook place in boiling salted water, with a little lemon juice. Generally, they are ready when the water returns to the boil or when they turn pink. Cool with cold water, place in the refrigerator
- lots of fresh crisp lettuce, washed dried and chopped into strips
- lemon wedges

The sauce
- 4 tbsp mayonnaise
- 4 tbsp tomato ketchup
- ½ to 1 tps horseradish or wasabi (according to how strong you want it, but it ought to have a kick)
- good dash tabasco
- sprinkle of lemon juice
- salt and pepper to taste
- parsley for topping

Method
- Mix the sauce well except for the parsley, taste for seasoning and the horseradish.
- Chill the sauce for about 20 minutes.
- Add the prawns coating them well with this sauce.
- Place the lettuce on the base of the serving bowl or bowls, followed by the prawn mixture, sprinkle the parsley and place the lemon wedges on the side.

Serves 4

Fish paté

Again a healthier choice, use smoked fish if you prefer...

Ingredients

- 450 gm fish deboned and poached in some milk that has some onion in it. (About 10 minutes should do. Remove from the milk and let cool. Add to the fish
- 3 tbsp mayonnaise
- 3 tbsp double cream
- 1 clove garlic crashed
- 1 tsp brandy
- ½ lime juice
- 1 cup fresh breadcrumbs
- good dash Tabasco
- good dash anchovy essence (optional)
- salt and pepper to taste

Method

- Mix the above ingredients flaking the fish as you go. If you want it chunky, be a little gentle and if you want it finer go ahead and beat it with gusto, using a fork or blender.
- Place in small containers or one bowl, decorate with gherkins, olives and slices of lemon.
- Remember to check the seasoning. Serve with warm French bread, crackers or toast, as you like.

Serves 2 – 4

. . . .

Rosemary walnuts

Warm, toasty and very good for you, lovely with drinks or as a snack. You could use cashews too.

Ingredients

- 6 tbsp butter
- 1 tbsp dried rosemary
- ½ tsp cayenne
- 4 cups walnuts

Method
- Melt the butter on a medium heat, toss in the rest of the ingredients, mix well, remove from the heat and lay on a baking tray.
- Bake in an oven at 200°C for about 10 –15 minutes till light brown.
- Serve warm if possible.

Serves 4

. . . .

Apple chips

Slightly healthier than their cousins the famous potato crisps (chips).

Method
- Take 4 apples, thinly slice them on a mandolin, place on a baking tray and bake in a hot oven at 200°C for 1 hour or a little more till they are crisp.
- Dust with icing sugar and serve.

Serves 2

. . . .

Cool avocado mousse

Refreshing and amazingly simple, yet very addictive. We have such heavenly avocados here!

Ingredients

- 1 cucumber, peeled, cut in half, seeds removed, cubed and salted with ½ tsp of salt, let sit on a sieve for 20 minutes to let the excess water drain. Rinse and pat dry, set aside
- 1 red, ripe tomato, deseeded and cubed, set aside with the cucumber
- 4 large avocados, peeled and stoned
- ½ a pint of double cream
- juice of one lemon
- 2 tbsp gelatine (or equivalent of leaf gelatine)
- salt, pepper, dash tabasco, dash lea and perrins (according to taste)

Method
- Blend the avocado, lemon, cream and seasoning.
- Dissolve the gelatine in some hot water (about under a cup full) add to the mixture, add the cucumber and tomato, adjust the seasoning, pour into a lightly greased mould or bowl (use olive oil).

- Place in the refrigerator and let set.
- To unmold you may have to place the container for a few moments in some hot water...not for long. You may also use smaller individual bowls.
- Serve with some warmed baguette or Melba toast.

Serves 4

. . . .

Kenya fish and coconut soup

A truly Kenyan product that reflects our beautiful country.

Ingredients

- 1 coconut shredded
- 1 kg sea fish or chicken
- 1 can coconut milk
- a little oil
- 3 onions finely diced
- 2 tsp cumin
- 1 tsp garlic
- 1 tsp ginger
- 1 litre chicken stock skimmed
- 2 bunches coriander chopped
- dash lime juice
- salt and pepper to taste

Method

- Fry the onions till clear, about 10 minutes, sauté the chicken (if using fish, add at the end) add the cumin, garlic and ginger, continue to fry for about 4 minutes more, add the stock, shredded coconut, coconut milk, season well,
- Add lime juice and some chilli if you like.
- Just before serving, add the coriander.
- For that extra touch, you may cut some bread into cubes, coat lightly with some good olive oil, bake in a hot oven (at 200°C for about 10 minutes or till nicely browned float on the soup and ... enjoy).

Serves 4

. . . .

Sukuma wiki soup

Sukuma wiki is a kind of spinach that we eat in Kenya that is reasonable in price and delicious. The name implies that we are pushing the week . . .

Ingredients

- a little olive oil or whatever you have
- 500 gm *sukuma wiki* or spinach of your choice, finely chopped
- 2 onions finely chopped
- 4 tomatoes grated finely and some garlic according to your taste
- 1 l chicken stock
- 200 gm minced meat, seasoned well and made into tiny balls
- salt, pepper and some chilly, according to your taste

Method

- Heat the oil in a pan.
- Add the onions and fry till golden, add the tomatoes, garlic.
- Continue to sauté till tomatoes are a little soft, adding the sukuma wiki, with seasoning, kind of stir fry briefly, add the stock and simmer.
- Add your meat balls (you may actually add chicken, beef or even bits of Indian paneer (hard cheese like feta).
- If you need a really smooth soup, then you may liquidize it prior to adding the meatballs or chicken, etc. It will send ripples of joy through your family!

Serves 4

. . . .

Homemade muesli

It is fresher, wholesome, cheaper and better than those factory packs. This recipe is for two, so multiply by the portions required. Also add other fruit like grapes, oranges, mangos, passion, and pineapple. We have an abundance of fabulous fruit in Kenya.

Ingredients

- 1 cup rolled oats, toasted slightly under the grill and soaked in apple juice or orange juice for a few minutes … Add
- 2-3 tbsp honey
- juice of 1 lime
- ¼ cup fresh coconut flakes
- ½ a cup strawberries or fruit of your choice
- ½ cup toasted almonds or cashews
- 1 peeled apple, cored and grated or sliced
- ½ cup sultanas plumped up in some warm water for 15 minutes (drained)
- good sprinkling of lightly roasted nuts (pistachios cashews, almonds, etc.)
- ice cold milk, to serve with (or good Greek or organic yoghurt.)

Hint: If you are on diet, omit the honey and add your sweetener. For even a fruiter kick, add some good quality strawberry or rasberry jam.

Serves 2

. . . .

Fluffy souffle omelette . . . savoury or sweet as you wish

A light omelette that rises amazingly, the yolks and whites are beaten separately, heated in a pan and finished off under the grill. Have your grill on full. You may fill the omelette with sautéed mushrooms and onions, asparagus, ham, etc. Serve on warmed plates and eat right away as otherwise it will sink and that will not be fun!

Ingredients

- 4 eggs separated (the bowls must be spanking clean and no grease around)
- season the yolks with salt and pepper
- 1½ tbsp unsalted butter

Method

- Beat the egg yolk till frothy and season with salt and pepper.
- In a separate bowl beat the egg whites till stiff.
- Fold the egg white into the beaten yolk . . . let as much air in and fold, do not mix. It should be as light as possible.
- Place a pan on moderate heat and melt the butter and add the egg. When just set, cover handle of pan with foil and place under grill, and let rise.
- Add the filling of your choice and serve right away, on warmed plates. You can add sugar instead of salt in the egg yolk according to taste and fill with quality jam, fresh raspberries, and strawberries, lightly mashed or cut thinly, and lightly dusted with icing sugar. Some canned fruit like cherries, peaches diced and pears go well. This is a dainty tasty dish sure to flatter your family and friends.

Serves 4

Frittata with spinach, red pepper, potatoes and fresh coriander

The Kenyan version of a versatile omelette, that can be eaten at breakfast hot, or at any time you are hungry, cold on picnics and as a snack. Vary the ingredients as to what you may have in the refrigerator – cooked carrots, peas, leeks, etc.

Ingredients

- 6 eggs
- 3 tbsp olive oil

- 1 small bunch spinach just blanched in hot salted water and cut into bits
- 1 red (bell) pepper, chopped into tiny squares and blanched in boiling water. Simply place in a bowl, pour hot water over the peppers, leave to stand for 5 minutes, drain and rinse with cold water.
- 1 large potato boiled with skin on for 18 minutes or till just done, peeled and cubed
- 1 bunch fresh coriander leaves chopped, or parsley or chives
- 1 tbsp chopped basil
- salt and pepper to taste
- some good melting cheese to sprinkle at the end

Method

- Beat the eggs well and fold in the rest of the ingredients, except the olive oil and cheese. In a non-stick pan over medium heat, pour the olive oil in.
- Meanwhile, turn the grill on full too.
- Add the egg mixture and cover for about 4 minutes.
- Pull the side of the frittata away from the pan and let the runny egg fill it in and cook for another 1 minute.
- Cover the handle of your pan with foil and place under grill till nicely golden brown, add the cheese and give it a moment to melt.
- Serve at once.

Hint: Once the main ingredients are ready and they can be done well in advance the rest takes just moments. As I said earlier use any handy cooked ingredients that you may find suitable, I think even cooked soft corn might be nice. Experiment and you will be surprised at the end product that everyone will love over and over.

Serves 4

. . . .

Frittata with spinach, mushroom and red pepper

I have added nuts to this for a little texture and to make it more East African. An omelette on the go. Lovely eaten hot or cold. You may add cooked asparagus, potatoes, ham or whatever you fancy in small quantities though. These dishes were created also to 'use' up leftovers in the refrigerator or store, creating a new wonderful dish at no additional expense.

Ingredients

- 3 tbsp extra virgin olive oil
- 6 mushrooms washed, sliced thinly (they tell you not to wash mushrooms and to just wipe them. The Nairobi mud defeats this reasoning!)

- 1 large bell pepper seeded and cubed
- 1 tsp cumin
- 150 gm young spinach washed, dried and cut
- salt and pepper to taste
- 3 tbsp chopped cashews
- 5 eggs beaten and 1 tbsp of double cream mixed in
- 2 tsp chopped parsley
- 50 gm grated cheddar

Method

- In a large pan over medium heat add the olive oil, followed by the mushrooms and bell pepper. Sauté this for 5 minutes.
- Add the cumin and 2 minutes later throw in the spinach, salt and pepper to taste, cashews and egg. Set your grill to high.
- Meanwhile, pull the edges of the omelette away from the side of the pan and let the runny bits go underneath.
- Cover the handle of the pan with tin foil if it is not oven/heat proof, sprinkle the parsley and grated cheese over and grill untill set to your liking.
- A practical perfect meal for kids and adults alike and makes a great take out meal too. A nice crisp green salad hits the spot right on.

Serves 4

. . . .

French toast ... breakfast fun

As kids we loved it, time has forgotten it and it is another revival recipe made fresh. It is wholesome, warming, have it with cinnamon and cardamom added for that East African touch, with marmite, or jam. Use brown bread and honey (1 tbsp) instead of sugar. The variety is unlimited.

Ingredients

In a bowl mix together
- 4 eggs
- 1 cup milk (or with a little double cream added to make a mix of milk and cream)
- 1 tbsp sugar or honey
- ½ tsp salt
- 1 tsp real vanilla essence
- good pinch cardamom (optional)
- good pinch cinnamon (optional)
Then...
- 4-5 slices of bread
- ½ tbsp butter and ½ tbsp olive oil (mixed or 1 tbsp butter)

Method

- Soak the bread in the egg mix, turning once, place a pan (non-stick is even better) on medium heat, add a little fat, let it froth up and place two slices at a time, till golden brown, turning, repeat the process.
- Eat as you make them for the best success, the chef has to sacrifice but can eat as he/she cooks away, that too can be fun.

Serves 4

....

Turbo smoothie

This gives you the energy needed for the day ... tofu is available in good supermarkets. Whizz in a blender till smooth. Encourage your kids to have smoothies instead of soft drinks.

Ingredients

- ½ a cup of tofu
- 1½ cup of peach or pear nectar
- ½ a cup of pineapple cubed
- ½ a cup of strawberries or raspberries diced
- 1 tsp lemon juice

Method

The idea of drinking tofu can take a little time to like, but once you do, there is no going back. You will enjoy.

....

Fresh fruit mix smoothie

Place in a blender till smooth. So much healthier for us.

Ingredients

- 2 cups cantaloupe or honey dew melon (deseeded, skin removed and cubed)
- 1 cup plain yoghurt
- 2 cups grapes (deseeded if you like)
- 1 tbsp fresh milk
- 1 tbsp lemon juice
- a drizzle of honey

Method

Chill and serve.

....

Morning smoothie

Refreshing, healthy, no additive, no added sugar, keep the fruit cold before blending. Place in a blender.

Ingredients

- 1 cup fresh orange juice
- 1 cup diced strawberries
- 1 cup pawpaw or pineapple diced
- 1 banana

Method

Blend till smooth, serve right away.

Serves 2

Carrot smoothie

Good for you and your eyes.

Ingredients

- 1 cup carrot juice (put fresh peeled carrots through juicer) then add in a blender together with the carrot juice
- 1 cup cubed fresh mango
- 1 cup diced strawberries
- good pinch fresh ginger

Method

Whizz in the blender till smooth, chill in the freezer for a few minutes ... do not forget it. Put your timer on.

Serves 2

Beetroot mix smoothie

How amazing can nature's goodness and colours be!

Ingredients

- ½ cup grated beetroot
- 1 cup carrot juice prepared as above in a juicer first
- 1 cup apple juice
- 1 tsp lime juice
- good pinch ginger

Method

Blend till smooth, chill and serve.

Serves 2

. . . .

Water melon smoothie

So cool.

Ingredients

- 1 water melon seeded and cut into chunks
- 130 ml plain Greek yoghurt

Method

Whizz in a blender till smooth, chill and ... wow! What a good start to the day!

Serves 2

. . . .

Caramelised grapefruit

A refreshing way to start the day or to have as a dessert. Adjust the sweetness according to your taste ... or simply add some fresh reduced orange juice instead.

Ingredients

- 2 grapefruit split in half, pips removed and cut into segments then removed (keep casing)
- 4 tbsp sweet sherry or port (optional)
- 3 tsp honey
- 4 tbsp brown sugar to sprinkle on top

Method

- Mix all the above except for the brown sugar.
- Replace into the casing and brown under a high grill.
- Remove once bubbling.
- Serve straight away.

Serves 4

. . . .

Passion, pawpaw and cantaloupe melon with port

An exciting way with two fantastic Kenyan fruits; again nice for breakfast or a soothing healthy dessert.

Ingredients

- 2 pawpaws split in half and deseeded
- 6 passion fruits, split in half and contents removed
- whipped cream; about 6 tbsp
- a good drizzle of honey at the end

Method

- Fill the cavity of the pawpaw with the passion fruit (which you may like to sweeten).
- Top with the whipped cream and drizzle with honey.
- Chill well and serve.

Serves 2 – 4

. . . .

Cantaloupe melon with port

A favourite of mine as it does put back the zing in life. Another Kenyan great.

Ingredients

- 1 cantaloupe melon or honey dew, cut in half and deseeded, then add into cavity
- 1 tsp of finely grated ginger
- 8 flaked almonds or cashews
- 4 tbsp of sweet port

Method

- Mix the ingredients lightly with a spoon, within the cavity, chill and serve. If you find the melon not sweet enough have some sugar or honey handy nearby, simply sprinkle or drizzle on the side.
- Sometimes the best things in life are simple.

. . . .

Oven baked eggs

Try organic eggs. An elegant way of presenting eggs. I will give you the basic way and you may add cheese, cooked spinach or some finely chopped tomato with basil. These would go into the ramekins. Small oven proof bowls first then the egg. Make some buttered toast points, and dip into the dish once cooked. A fabulous way to start the day together with some smoothie recipes that I shall provide.

Ingredients

- 4 buttered ramekin dishes, lined at the bottom with what you like (as above or even cooked ham, mushrooms, asparagus, etc.)
- 4 eggs (organic if possible) broken into the ramekins, keeping the yolk whole if possible)
- salt, pepper and paprika (optional) according to taste

- A good sprinkle of parmesan or cheddar cheese on top
- 4 tbsp double cream ...1 tbsp per ramekin, on top of the egg

Method
- Set the oven to 200°C.
- Place ramekins in a large baking tray and add about 3 cm of boiling water onto the tray and put into the oven.
- Bake for about 7 minutes or till set as you like. A simple, elegant and perfect way to start the day, yet warm and consoling too.

Hint: Increase eggs as needed, but only one in each ramekin.

Serves 4

. . . .

Grilled sausages with tomatoes
A truly Kenyan breakfast with a twist...

Ingredients

- 35 gm unsalted butter
- 2 onions chopped
- 1 kg tomatoes cut into chunks
- 3 celery sticks diced
- ½ tsp sugar
- salt and pepper to taste
- a dash of tabasco
- ¼ cup white wine
- 1 tsp tomato puree
- 10 basil leaves shredded by hand and added at the end

Method
- In a pan over medium heat, add the butter and then the onions, cook till clear, drop in the tomatoes and celery. Stir till softened but not mushy.
- Season with sugar, salt, pepper and Tabasco.
- Turn up the heat and add the wine, let evaporate, add 1 tsp of tomato puree and then the basil, keep warm.

For the sausages . . .
- turn your grill to high.
- 1 packet sausages of your choice split in half lengthwise.
- Grill them until done to your liking, most of the bad fat will drain away as you grill.
- Serve on a warmed plate with the tomatoes, to tempt children. Add some baked beans and a few French fries to dunk in the sauce. I think that you will approve of this idea ... at least I hope you do. Tuck in!

Serves 4

Creamy scrambled eggs with smoked salmon

The perfect start to a day, served with good brown bread, consoling to the tasks that lie ahead. Warm the plates for that extra comfort ... and do not overcook. Beat together lightly in a bowl.

Ingredients

- 8 eggs
- salt and pepper
- 60 gm butter
- 1 tbsp double cream
- 2 tsp fresh chives or spring onions
- 1 tbsp milk
  Set aside for now
  On 4 plates arrange
- 4 slices of brown bread, buttered
- place pieces of salmon on top of the bread

Method

- Place a large frying pan with about 2 cm of water in it on medium heat. When the water is hot, place a smaller pan on this pan with water.
- In the smaller pan, melt the butter, add the egg mixture and scramble away, till just setting (do not overcook).
- Place equal portions of this scrambled egg onto the ready plates and with a teaspoon add a little mayonnaise. Serve straight away. If for some reason you do not like salmon, cooked asparagus or artichoke hearts are lovely.

Serves 4

Breakfast pancakes

Simple to prepare, you can stack them up, as you go wrapped in foil and kept in a warm oven or serve as you go. These can be filled with jam, fresh fruit like chopped orange segments, bananas, apples topped with icing sugar, or like in Holland you crisp up a few rashers of bacon, pour the batter, overcook both sides and then dribble with some maple syrup, honey or golden syrup ... If too thin add some milk and do not despair if the shapes are odd it will come with practice . . . what fun!

Ingredients

Mix together, and then let rest for half an hour
- 180 gm plain sifted flour
- 2 eggs
- 455 ml milk
- pinch salt

Method

- If lumpy pass through a sieve, you will need some butter to grease the pan... about 30 gm butter (unsalted).

- Heat a frying pan about 20 cm wide on medium heat.
- Place a little butter and swirl it around, add about 4 tbsp of the batter and rotate° the pan so the batter spreads.
- Soon it will have some small holes, lift to see if browned, turn and repeat the process.
- Stack separating them with grease proof paper, cover with foil and keep warm.
- Try the variations above, or at lunch time fill them with some cooked buttered asparagus, or creamed spinach.
- Quite a sociable dish once the cooking is done and everyone gathers together for a treat.

Serves 4

· · · · · · · · · · · · · · · · · · · ·

Ken-ind omelette

As the name implies this is a Kenyan-Indian inspired recipe. We used to have it for breakfast on Sundays with parathas (Indian fried chapati), but good bread is equally nice. Somehow eaten cold when we went on picnics it still held its goodness. I think it has a place in our hearts.

Ingredients

In a bowl mix together:

- 4 eggs
- 1 onion chopped
- ¼ tsp red chilli
- 2 pinches salt
- 2 pinches pepper
- 1 green chilli chopped
- 2 tbsp freshly chopped dhania
- 2 tomatoes seeds removed and chopped
- 2 tbsp cream or milk
- butter for frying (do not mix with the above)

Method

- Place a frying pan on medium heat and put a good knob of butter in it (about 2 tbs). Pour the egg mixture in and let it set, carefully turn it over and cook the other side till done to your liking.
- Serve with toast, *parathas* and pickle.
- Once you have tried this, you will agree that it is utterly delicious and highly addictive.

Serves 2

· · · · · · · · · · · · · · · · · · · ·

Cheese straws

Another snack that has fallen out and still deserves a revival. It was a favourite at tea time and to some who looked in horror, it was sometimes lightly smeared with marmite.

Ingredients

- 1 cup plain flour, with a good pinch of salt, sieved
- ½ tsp mustard powder
- ½ cup butter
- ½ cup finely grated mature cheddar
- 1 tbsp parmesan
- 1 egg beaten

Method

- In a bowl, place the flour, mustard, and butter.
- Rub this mixture, till it becomes crumbly.
- Add the cheese (both), mixing with your hands, adding the egg slowly. It should be stiff.
- Refrigerate for about 20 minutes.
- Remove and put onto a floured board and knead till smooth.
- Roll out the pastry to about 1 cm thick, and cut into strips.
- Twist these strips, or some of them, brush with some milk, place on a greased baking tray and bake at 200° C for about 10 minutes or till they are golden brown.
- Let cool, served at tea time or sundowners, they are a taste of the 1960's. Dare you use the marmite on some?

Serves 2

. . . .

Mixed coleslaw

A slight slant on the usual coleslaw. The addition of apples and sultanas give this salad an exotic flavour. If pears are in season or you like grapes, add those too. Sometimes I even add some macadamia nuts for an added crunch.

Ingredients

- 1 green cabbage shredded, washed
- 2 cups red cabbage shredded, washed
- 5 stalks celery chopped
- 5 spring onions chopped
- 2 carrots grated
- 2 apples peeled, cored and cut into wedges, brushed with lemon juice
- handful of sultanas, plumped up in hot water for an hour

Dressing

- 1½ cups mayonaise
- 5 tbsp lemon juice

- ¼ cup sugar
- ½ tsp salt
- good sprinkle of pepper
- 1 tsp caraway seeds
- some freshly chopped parsley to beautify!

Method

- Place both cabbages into a bowl with ice cold water, leave for an hour, drain and squeeze out excess water.
- Put into a large bowl together with the rest of the ingredients except the dressing.
- Mix the dressing well, and add to the cabbage mix. Toss till dressed, check the seasoning; sprinkle some freshly chopped parsley, chill in the refrigerator, and remove when needed.
- Serve alongside your main course. The flavours of nature are featured in this interesting salad.

Serves 4

. . . .

Cocktail mushrooms

Get the freshest button mushrooms and these wonderful appetisers go well served alongside cubes of cheese with thin slithers of onions or on a cocktail stick with a kebab or a dainty sausage. Chunks of cucumber added complete the picture.

Ingredients

- 4 cups cider vinegar
- ½ cup lime juice
- 4 cloves of garlic halved
- 2 inch piece ginger in slithers
- 15 – 20 black pepper corns
- a good pinch mustard
- 2 bay leaves
- 2 sprigs thyme
- 3 red chillies minced
- 1 kg button mushrooms wiped over with a damp cloth

Method

- In a pan over high flame, mix in all the ingredients except for the mushrooms, bring to boil, reduce heat and simmer for 15 minutes.
- Then add the mushrooms, and continue to simmer for a further 10 minutes… uncovered.
- Cool and refrigerate till needed. You may like them spicy so add more chilli and some toasted cumin. The end result is a product far superior and tastier then the canned version.

Serves 4 – 6

Cooling spinach raita

Our local spinach is super delicious. A clever side dish that is a salad as well as a palate cooler.

Ingredients

- 2 cups spinach, cleaned and chopped finely
- 1 cup cabbage cleaned and chopped finely
- ½ cup carrots julienned
- I cup thick yoghurt
- salt and red chilli to taste
  For the tempering:
- 3 tbsp oil
- 1 tsp mustard seeds
- 1 tsp cumin seeds

Method

- To temper, place the oil in a pan and over high heat, add the mustard seeds, they will begin to splatter.
- Add the cumin seeds, followed by the vegetables, stir fry for about 3 minutes, cool. If there is too much liquid drain it, add the yoghurt and seasoning.
- Put into a serving bowl and top with some chopped fresh dhania and a sprinkle of garam masala. Cool.
- Serve alongside with nyama choma, curries and stews.

Serves 4

. . . .

Oriental slaw

A slant on the usual cabbage recipe ... use local cashews or even peanuts instead of pine nuts. Some freshly shredded coconut adds to the exotic flavour.

Ingredients

- 1 medium cabbage, thinly sliced, blanched in boiling water and then rinsed with cold water and then excess water squeezed out gently
- ½ a cup freshly shredded coconut
- ½ a cup green pepper, sliced and blanched
- ½ a cup finely shredded carrots
- 2 tbsp lightly toasted sesame seeds (place in a dry pan and toast over medium heat till lightly golden)
- 4 tbsp red wine vinegar
- 1 tsp sesame oil
- 3 tsp good olive oil
- 2 tsp sugar

- ½ tsp salt
- freshly milled black pepper
- chilli to taste
- pine nuts or cashews, toasted and added at the very last minute

Method

- Mix all the above ingredients well except for the nuts.
- Chill, then taste and adjust seasoning.
- Add nuts.

Serves 4

. . . .

Tsavo cabbage

Aptly named as the cabbage, it turns a slightly brown colour like the soil there. I had this at a lodge and have tried to recreate it to the best of my ability. Some chefs are reluctant to part with their closely guarded secrets and it took me a while to perfect this.

Ingredients

- 1 cabbage shredded and washed
- ¼ cup oil
- 4 tbsp butter
- ¼ cup basalmic vinegar (or white wine vinegar)
- ½ a cup apple juice
- 3 – 4 tbsp honey
- a handful of cashews chopped roughly
- salt and pepper to taste

Method

- Heat the oil and butter till browned a little bit, throw in the cabbage and sauté for about 12 minutes, add the rest of the ingredients except the cashews, salt and pepper, to be added at the end.
- Towards the end of cooking if there is too much liquid, increase the heat to reduce some of the liquid. Great with all kinds of roasts, steaks and even sausages – kids love it.

Serves 4

. . . .

Lamu salad

Served very cold, it is sure to beat the heat and calm your nerves as you look out to the ocean with some chilled wine at hand.

Ingredients

- a hand full of sultanas, plumped up in a mug of warm water (for 20 minutes)
- 2 cucumbers seeded, cut into bite size chunks, salted for 20 minutes (1 tsp salt) then rinsed
- 2 ripe pawpaw, seeded, peeled and cubed
- juice of one lime
- 2 fillets of fish, cooked and cubed (poach in water for about 7 minutes)
- 20 large or medium shrimp, cooked, peeled and deveined (boil in salted water with lemon till they turn pink)
- 4 tbsp mayonnaise
- lots of shredded lettuce
- salt and pepper to taste
- 2 spring onions sliced and one fresh coconut, split and flesh shredded as garnish

Method

- Simply mix all the ingredients together except for the spring onions and shredded coconut (add at the end) checking the seasoning and correcting it.
- Do not mush up the pawpaw. For added zing, add a little more lime and good pinch of cayenne pepper. Relax, and truly enjoy the tropical treasure.

Serves 4

. . . .

Alan Bobbe's aubergine (eggplant) recipe

Appropriately named after him, it is taken from one of Alan Bobbe's radio broadcasting tapes recorded in the early 1960's.

Ingredients

- 4 aubergines, cut in half and the flesh scooped out (save shell)
- 1 cup chopped pork or beef fillet
- 2 cloves garlic crushed
- 1 small onion chopped
- 1 cup mushrooms sliced
- 4 anchovy fillets mashed up
- 2 slices of bread moistened with a bit of white wine
- 1 egg beaten
- salt and pepper to taste and a dash Tabasco
- ½ a cup parmesan cheese grated finely
- 1 lemon

Method

- Mix all the ingredients together except for the lemon. Replace in the shell and bake for 40 minutes or so at 200°C, sprinkle the lemon juice, adjust seasoning, replace in oven for 5 minutes and serve.
- Serve with hot garlic bread, and a salad.

Serves 4

....

Beetroot – like you never knew

A interesting way to cook a vegetable that not all of us like. Probably because its prepared like hospital food in most restaurants, this may entice you to like it.

Ingredients

- 6 beetroots, cleaned, cooked in the oven for about an hour at 200°C, then peeled. Cut into chunks
- 50 gm butter
- 4 tbsp honey
- 2 lemons squeezed
- 2 onions finely chopped
- dash tabasco
- salt and pepper

Method

- Melt the butter and add the onions. Fry till clear – 5 minutes or so.
- Add the honey lemon, tabasco, salt and pepper.
- Let the sauce thicken a bit and add the beetroots.
- Heat through and serve. It is really good with cold cuts, sandwiches, or even a salad, mixed with lettuce of your choice and cucumbers and onions.

Serves 4

....

Vichyssoise

An old favourite revived.

Ingredients

- 4 potatoes, peeled, washed and chopped
- 6 leeks, sliced and washed in several changes of water
- 2 onions, chopped
- 300 ml (½ pint) milk
- 300 ml (½ pint) cream
- 2 tbsp corn flour
- 1½ tsp butter
- 1 l (35 fl oz) hot water

- ½ cup dry white wine
- 2 chicken stock cubes
- chopped chives to garnish
- salt and pepper to taste

Method

- Sauté the leeks, onions and potatoes in the butter over a medium flame for 10 minutes.
- Add the hot water, wine and stock cubes and simmer for 15 minutes. Allow it to cool a little and pour through a sieve.
- Replace in the pan.
- Meanwhile, mix together the milk, cream and corn flour and add it to the ingredients in the pan.
- Replace the pan on the fire and heat through but do not allow to boil.
- Season, chill well and garnish with chopped chives when ready to serve.

Serves 4

. . . .

Avocado Frédérique

A favourite at the Café Frédérique which I managed in The Netherlands.

Ingredients

- 2 avocados, halved, stoned and pureed and immediately mixed with 2 tbsp lime juice. (Reserve the avocado shells)
- 4 slices of beef bacon, fried till crisp and then crumbled
- 1 onion, finely sliced
- 1 bunch of dhania, chopped
- 1 tbsp Worcestershire sauce
- 1 tsp tabasco
- 1 tsp soya sauce
- 2 tbsp brandy
- salt and freshly ground pepper
- parsley to garnish

Method

- Mix all the ingredients with the puréed avocado.
- Season to suit your taste.
- Replace into the reserved shells or use a glass bowl lined with some lettuce.
- Chill well and top with parsley before serving.

Serves 4

Joanna salad

Aptly named after a friend at Le Jardin hotel (now closed down).

Ingredients

- 3 avocados, peeled, sliced and sprinkled with lime juice
- 2 cucumbers, peeled, seeded and thinly sliced
- 3 tomatoes, washed, seeded and sliced
- 20 medium prawns, washed, de-veined and cooked
- 1 tin tuna (in oil) drained
- tettuce, washed
  Arrange all the ingredients on a platter. Chill.
  For the dressing:
- 1½ cups mayonnaise (see glossary)
- 2 cloves garlic, crushed
- 1 tbsp brandy
- 1 tbsp lime juice
- ¼ tsp mustard
- ¼ tsp mixed herbs
- 1 bunch spring onions, finely chopped
- 2 tbsp tomato ketchup
- a little tabasco
- 1 bunch spring onions, finely chopped
- salt and freshly milled pepper
- parsley

Method

- Mix all the ingredients for the dressing, leaving a little parsley to garnish.
- Check seasoning. When ready to serve, pour the dressing over the salad according to your preference.
- Top with the remaining parsley.

Serves 4

· · · · · · · · · · · · · · · · · · · ·

Avocado salad

By now you know how mighty our avocados are!

Ingredients

- 3 medium ripe avocados
- 1 green pepper, seeded, blanched and sliced
- 3 tomatoes, seeded, sliced
- *1 cup cooked couscous (available at supermarkets)
- 200 gm (7 oz) snow-peas (mange-tout), blanched or young French beans, blanched
- ½ cup blanched almonds, skinned and chopped coarsely

- 2 bunches spring onions, chopped
  For the dressing:
- 1 tbsp mustard
- ½ cup oil (mix olive oil and salad oil)
- 2 tbsp lime juice
- ¼ tbsp mixed herbs
- 1 clove garlic, crushed
- salt and pepper to taste

Method

- Mix all the ingredients together except the avocado, which should be peeled, seeded and sliced and added when you are ready to serve.
- As an extra, a little crisped beef bacon or ½ a cup de-veined, cleaned, cooked prawns can be added.

Hint: The best way to cook couscous is by boiling it like rice for 15 minutes with salt. Add a little butter, drain in a sieve and cool. Fluff up with a fork.

Serves 4

. . . .

Kilifi crab salad

Ingredients

- 4 medium-sized crabs (cooked). If live, plunge into boiling water for 20 minutes
- 1 cucumber, peeled, seeded and sliced
- 1 avocado, peeled, sliced and coated with lime juice
- 2 tomatoes, seeded and chopped
- 1 head crisp lettuce
- 2 bunches spring onions, chopped (optional)
- 1½ cups mayonnaise
- ½ tsp grain mustard
- 4 tbsp dry white wine
- salt and freshly milled pepper to taste

Method

- Crack the claws of the crab and remove the flesh.
- Open the body shell; discard the stomach, grey fingers and other "techni-coloured" parts, leaving just the white flesh.
- Mix the crab meat with the mayonnaise, mustard, cucumber and wine.
- Season.
- Replace the mixture into the shell or into glass bowls.
- Decorate with avocado, tomato, lettuce and top with spring onions if liked.
- Chill and serve.

Serves 4 – 6

Nakuru corn salad

Ingredients

- 2 tins corn off the cob
- 1 onion sliced in fine strips
- 1 bunch spring onions, chopped
- 4 tomatoes, washed, seeded and sliced
- 1 cos lettuce, washed,
- ½ a cup freshly grated coconut
- parsley to garnish
  Dressing
- 1¾ tbsp white wine vinegar
- juice of 1 lime
- 2 tbsp olive oil, 2 tbsp salad oil
- 2 cloves garlic, crushed
- salt and freshly milled pepper

Method

- Drain the corn in a sieve and pour boiling water over it. Repeat.
- Mix the ingredients for the dressing well.
- In a glass bowl, place all the other ingredients except for the lettuce and parsley. Toss them together.
- Before serving, arrange the lettuce around the bowl, add the dressing and garnish with the parsley.

Hint: If wine vinegar is not available, you may substitute with malt vinegar.

Serves 4

....

Greek salad

Our Kenyan feta is very good!

Ingredients

- 500 gm (1 lb) feta cheese
- 4 tomatoes, washed, seeded and sliced neatly
- 1 cucumber, peeled, seeded and sliced
- ¼ kg (9 oz) French beans, cooked
- ½ cup macadamia or pine nuts
- ½ bunch cooked asparagus
- 10 olives
- 4 small gherkins
- ¼ tsp basil
- 2 spring onions, finely chopped
- 1 cos lettuce, washed well
- ½ cup fresh mushrooms, washed (using water and vinegar), sliced

For the dressing:
- ½ cup olive oil (plain or mixed with corn oil)
- ½ cup wine vinegar
- juice of 2 limes
- 2 cloves garlic, crushed
- 2 tbsp chopped dill
- ¼ tsp mustard
- salt and freshly milled pepper to taste

Method

- Cut the cheese carefully into small cubes.
- Place all the other ingredients neatly or according to your preference.
- Mix all the ingredients for the dressing together and add to the salad just before serving.

Hint: Sometimes the feta cheese available is crumbly. Avoid this type. Go for the type which is in medium-sized blocks.

Serves 4

Garlic mushrooms
So addictive!

Ingredients

- 1 punnet small button mushrooms, washed and left in water with a little vinegar for 5 minutes
- 6 tbsp butter
- 9 cloves garlic, crushed
- 1½ tbsp lime juice
- parsley
- salt and pepper to taste

Method

- Melt butter in a pan then add the mushrooms and sauté.
- When the mushrooms begin to "sweat," increase the heat to high.
- Add the garlic and lime juice.
- When all the liquid has evaporated, season and garnish.
- Serve with warm bread.

Serves 4

Fried camembert and parsley

Delicious, different – and messy! Again the local camembert is very good.

Ingredients

- 2 very cold discs camembert cheese (not too "ripe"), cubed
- 2 eggs, well beaten
- breadcrumbs, seasoned with salt and pepper
- plenty of vegetable oil for deep-frying
- 3 bunches parsley, trimmed

Method

- Dip the cheese in the egg mixture and then in the breadcrumbs.
- Refrigerate for 10 minutes.
- Repeat this twice.
- Heat the oil for deep-frying.
- Try one block of cheese first.
- It should brown quickly without "leaking".
- Carry on adding the rest of the camembert slowly until you get the hang of it – you get the best results by frying just a few blocks at a time. Once all the cheese is done, deep-fry the parsley in the same way but without coating it – making sure it is completely dry before placing it in the oil.
- When crisp it's ready. This recipe will probably finish off all your oil, but it's definitely worth the effort!
- Eat it quickly to get the full benefit of the flavour.

Serves 6

. . . .

Nakuru-style corn on the cob

A somewhat different way of cooking corn, taught to me by my aunt Shamin, an excellent cook. You must be careful when trying out this recipe. It can be dangerous if you are using high heat, as the corn may pop.

Ingredients

- 4 medium-sized soft corn cobs, husked
- 1 cup vegetable oil
- 5 tbsp butter
- salt and pepper
- lime juice

Method

- Heat the oil and butter in a frying pan over a low to medium flame.
- Place the corn cobs, whole, in the oil and let them sauté slowly.
- It is a good idea to remove the pan from the fire whilst turning the corn.
- Turn the corn constantly as each side turns a light brown.
- When all the corn is brown, it is done.
- Remove from the pan and season with salt, pepper and a few drops of lime juice.

. . . .

Hot grapefruit

A simple, refreshing starter.

Ingredients

- 2 grapefruits, pipped and segments cut out (keep casing)
- 4 tbsp sweet sherry
- 2 tsp honey
- 1 – 2 tsp sugar
- 1 tsp unsalted butter, frozen and diced
- mint leaves to garnish

Method

- Mix the grapefruit segments with the butter, sherry and honey.
- Replace into casing, sprinkle with sugar and place under a moderately hot grill until the sugar browns slightly.
- Decorate with mint leaves.

Hint: If it is not possible to reserve the casing neatly, you may put the segments into small pyrex bowls.

Serves 4

. . . .

Melon cocktail

Very handy for an impressive, quick starter when friends land in your home without warning.

Ingredients

- 2 honey-clew melons sliced in ½, de-seeded and diced (keep casing)
- ½ cup sweet sherry/port
- pinch fresh ginger
- crushed mint leaves to garnish

Method

- Mix the sherry with the ginger and gently spoon the mixture over the diced.
- Place everything in the melon casings and chill.
- Decorate with the mint before serving.

Hint: Either cantaloupe or water melon can be used. Use a spoon to scoop the melon flesh. If you prefer, you can serve the cocktail in small pyrex bowls instead of the melon casing. A few slices of cooked, crispy beef bacon or smoked beef, finely chopped, can also be added.

Serves 4

. . . .

Chapter 3

Chicken

Southern fried chicken

An addictive recipe that one has to learn to use only as comfort food, given that fried food is so very tasty yet not so very good for our waist. However everything in small doses is allowed, I think, so here we go …

Ingredients

- 1 large chicken or 12 pieces of chicken (rub over with yoghurt and let it rest for 1 hour
- mix in a bowl (referred to as the mix later)
- 1 tsp thyme
- 1 tsp oregano
- 7 tsp paprika
- 6 tsp celery salt
- 6 tsp onion salt
- 3 tsp mustard powder
- 1 tsp cayenne pepper
- ½ tsp salt
- good grind of freshly milled pepper

Method
- Divide this mix into three separate little bowls.
- Sprinkle one bowl of the mix over the chicken and let it rest for at least an hour.

Next you will need:
- 1 kg flour (½ kg corn flour and ½ kg home baking flour)
- 3 eggs beaten
- oil for deep frying

Method
- Sprinkle the second bowl of the mix into the flour and the third bowl of mix into the beaten egg.
- Heat the oil, test if ready by dropping a small piece of bread into it. It should rise to the top quickly and brown.
- Reduce the heat just a little.
- Dip the pieces of chicken into the egg, coating it well and then coat it comfortably with the flour.
- Place on a tray that also has been sprinkled with a little flour.
- Fry the chicken in batches; it should take about 15 minutes. If it is cooking too fast, reduce the heat.

- Check when golden brown to see when if cooked through by pricking it. The liquid that comes out should be clear.
- Keep warm as you prepare the rest.
- Serve with mashed potatoes, green salad, and coleslaw or even dare I say French fries.

Hint: If the chicken does cook too fast remove the pan from the heat for a few minutes, and reduce the heat slightly. Then, put back on the heat. Like all good tasty foods, this is addictive and comforting and once in a while we do need comfort.

Serves 4 – 6

. . . .

Tandoori chicken . . . needs time to marinate

A sister to the famous chicken tika, equally as good but usually on the bone, so use plump chickens.....not the sad variety most restaurants here tend to throw onto our plates at inflated prices. We bake these in the oven till just done, succulent and aromatic it is the ultimate in tandoori cooking and loved by the young and old alike. Place all these marinade ingredients in a blender and wizz till smooth

Ingredients

- 2 cups plain thick yoghurt (if too runny put in a clean muslin cloth over a sieve and let it drain for 45 minutes.)
- 3 tsp fresh ginger (cut into segments)
- 4 cloves garlic crushed
- 3 green chillies (more or less according to taste)
- 1 bunch fresh coriander leaves (dhania)
- 1¼ tsp salt
- ½ tsp red chilli powder
- 1 tsp ground cumin (pound whole cumin to powder)
- 1 tsp ground coriander powder
- 1 tsp garam masala
- 2 tsp lemon juice
- 2 tbsp corn oil (any good oil ... not olive this time)
- healthy pinch saffron or ½ tsp turmeric

Method

- Place this tandoori marinade in a bowl and set aside for now.
- 1 large chicken quarter, or 4 portions, breast or leg, skin removed.
- Slash the flesh so that the marinade can really sink in.
- Place the chicken pieces in the marinade and place in the refrigerator for the night. (Two nights is good too but not essential).

- Remove from the fridge about hour before use.
- Put your oven on 200° C and place chicken on a tray.
- Bake this for about 20 minutes, test to see if done.
- Prick the leg with a skewer and if the liquid is clear it is done … or just tear a bit of the meat from the thickest part of the leg and see if cooked through.
- Serve with a coriander-mint dip, (recipe follows) warmed buttery pitta bread and a nice crunchy green salad.
- Now here is a meal that will make you think twice about eating it out at twice the cost and half the flavour.

· · · · · · · · · · · · · · · · · · · ·

Coriander mint dip
What would we do without the mighty dhania?

Ingredients

- 1 cup thick plain yoghurt (if not thick, place a cloth over a sieve and let drip)
- 1 bunch mint leaves
- 1 big bunch fresh coriander (dhania)
- 2 green chillies (more if you like it hot)
- ½ a tsp salt
- sprinkle of garam masala at the end

Method
- Whizz this in a small blender, check seasoning, sprinkle garam masala on top and refrigerate till needed.
- As an extra treat, make double the quantity and add a tsp of freshly ground ginger into one of them. They will be transformed into two entirely different dips.

Hint: My grandmother used to pound the mint, coriander and chilli in mortar and pestle, patiently to a smooth paste and then add the yoghurt and mix energetically. Those were the days of no electrical blenders. The two sauces are shockingly good and again put to shame what some restaurants serve us here.

Serves 4

· · · · · · · · · · · · · · · · · · · ·

Cheats chicken curry
Use this only when you have little time. It is quick, simple and a bit like the colonial curries we used to get in the 1960's. May be it brings back that waft we so got used to every Sunday in those days. Served with sweet, hot mango chutney, rice and nan bread, you have conjured up a feast in no time.

Ingredients

- 1 chicken cut up into pieces (skin removed if you wish)
- 5 green chillies finely chopped
- 1 tbsp crushed garlic
- 1 tbsp ginger crushed
- 1 tsp cumin powder
- 1 onion finely chopped
- 1 can tomatoes chopped
- ½ tsp tumeric
- 1 can coconut cream
- 400 ml water
- salt to taste

Method

- Place all the ingredients in a pan and steadily bring to the boil, lower the heat to simmer. The sauce should just sort of blup ... blup.
- Check after 40 minutes to see if done.
- Correct the seasoning if need be.
- Remove from heat, place in a serving dish and add:
    - 3 tbsp lemon juice(stir)
    - 4 peeled boiled eggs
    - 1 bunch chopped fresh coriander
    - good sprinkle of garam masala.
- Serve as I mentioned above.
- For some strange reason I prefer this with slightly mushy, overcooked rice, sometimes with added frozen sweet peas and a sour mango pickle.
- Try it, there is a definite marriage here with no sign of divorce ever!

Serves 4

. . . .

Chicken palak ... great sukuma

Prepare all the ingredients in advance and line them up in bowls. That is half the work done and the rest is fun to prepare and good to eat. You can use Italian spinach or sukuma wiki too. This spinach is one of my favourite ways of serving. Prepare one day ahead and the flavour will really improve.

Ingredients

- 15 bunches palak, cleaned and 3 bunches of coriander cleaned. (Blanch the two in boiling water for 4 minutes, puree in a food processor and set aside for now).
- 1 chicken cut into portions (beef or lamb can be used)
  - ¼ cup oil
  - 6 onions finely chopped
  - 1 tbsp cumin powder
  - 2 tsp coriander powder
  - 4 sticks cinnamon
  - 5 cloves
  - 4 tbsp crushed garlic
  - 4 tbsp grated ginger
  - ½ tsp red chilli
  - 6 chopped tomatoes
  - 1 cup chicken stock
  - 4 tsp *methi* (fenugreek) ... dried is available at Indian ration stores
  - ½ cup double cream
  - a good sprinkle of garam masala
  - 2 bunches fresh coriander chopped
  - salt and pepper to taste

Method

- In a large pan, sauté the chicken till evenly browned (it will cook more later). Remove the chicken and reserve.
- In the same oil, brown the onions, then add the cumin, coriander powder, cinnamon sticks and cloves, stir well and continue to add the ginger, garlic and chilli.
- Place the tomatoes in the pan and sauté till soft, add the stock, simmer and return the chicken to the pot, cook till nearly done about 15 minutes, add the fenugreek and the spinach, coriander mix, stir the double cream in, sprinkle garam masala and fresh coriander.
- Season well.
- Serve with rice and bread, chapati or moist ugali. As an extra treat temer the spinach with added garlic (4 cloves) and the same amount of ginger, topped with some fenugreek *(methi)*. Absolutely fab ... if you are vegetarian, use paneer, a hard feta like cheese or plain is good too ... *karibu*.

Serves 4

. . . .

Chicken burgers with a chilli dip

A brother to the mighty beef burger, this version is slightly spicier and good for you too. The meat once mixed needs to rest a while so that the flavours can develop. The result is one tasty juicy burger. Mix in a bowl and let it rest for an hour. Moto moto sauce.

Ingredients

- 300 gm chicken mince
- 1 slice of bread grated
- 1 egg
- 1 bunch fresh coriander
- 3 cloves garlic crushed
- 1 tbsp ginger crushed
- 1 tbsp soy sauce
- 1 green chilli chopped
- 2 onions finely chopped, fried in a little oil, till clear, drain on kitchen paper and add to this mix.
- ¼ tsp salt
- ½ tsp freshly ground pepper

Method

- Form into little mini burgers. Wet your hands frequently as it helps make the shape.
- Fry in oil for about 5 minutes each side, drain on kitchen paper, keep warm and serve with chilli dip . . .

Chilli dips

Moto moto sause

Ingredients

- 100 ml water
- 4 – 5 red chillies chopped (finely)
- 100 gm sugar
- salt

Method

- In a pan over high heat, add the water and sugar, let it boil, reduce heat to medium, keep stirring till it turns thick and syrup like.
- Add the chopped chilli and remove from heat (this could take as much time as half an hour. Add salt according to taste, chill.
- Serve on their own or in fresh warm hamburger bread with mayo, crisp lettuce, cucumber and the chilli dip.
- Quite simply one of the most delicious burgers I know of.

Serves 2

Chicken teriyaki

Moto moto sauce. A sweet garlicky dish with a twist as far as cooking goes, for you place it in the oven and you will have lots of time to do other things. This recipe is for 12 people, so you either have a party or decide to eat leftovers the next day. Either way it is well worth it. It does need marinating overnight though.

Ingredients

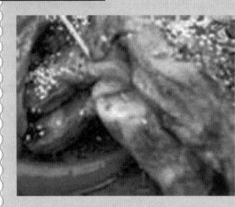

- 25 chicken pieces
- Marinade (mix in a pan and boil, remove from heat)
- 8 cups soy sauce
- 4 cups water
- 3 cups sugar
- 2 onions halved
- 4 cloves garlic crushed
- 4 cm piece of ginger, whole
- 1 cup white wine
- ½ tsp black pepper

Method

- Cool the marinade and then place the chicken pieces in.
- Refrigerate overnight, remove from the refrigerator an hour before use.
- Preheat the oven at 190°C, place the chicken pieces on a tray, leaving the marinade behind, and bake for about 45 minutes.
- Baste with the marinade every 20 minutes.
- Serve with rice, or buttery warm pitta bread. A wonderful recipe and one of the all time favourites.

Serves 12 – 15

....

Coriander chicken ... kuku dhania

Pretty simple to make and equally delicious, the coriander makes it look like a spinach dish with a difference.

Ingredients

- 5 chicken breasts, cubed and marinated
  Marinate
- 1 tsp garlic crushed
- 1 tsp ginger crushed
- 2 cups fresh coriander pounded
- 2 onions grated
- 2 tsp cumin powder

- 1 tsp turmeric
- 4 tbsp oil
- 1 tsp sugar
- 1 tsp red chilli
- 4 crushed tomatoes
- 1 tsp tomato puree

Method

- Let the chicken marinate in this for about 2 hours.
- In a large pan, add extra oil, drain as much of the liquid part of the marinade and add to the pan.
- Gradually add the chicken on medium heat.
- Add a little water, if too dry.
- Simmer on low flame for 15 minutes and add
  - 2 tbsp double cream
  - a good sprinkle of garam masala
  - 1 bunch fresh coriander chopped
  - 15 cashew nuts ground
- Stir well, check seasoning, and serve with rice and bread or ugali.

Serves 4

. . . .

Chicken kebab

Using chicken mince, these tender kebabs prove a healthy alternative to red meat and are ever so tasty.

Ingredients

- 1 kg chicken mince
- 1 tbsp cumin powder
- ¼ cup cashew nuts pounded
- ½ cup onions, first fried till clear and then added
- 3 tbsp oil
- 4 tsp ginger paste
- 3 tsp garlic paste
- 4 tbsp fresh coriander chopped
- 1 tsp garam masala
- 2 eggs beaten
- ½ tsp cardamom powder

Method

- Mix the above ingredients well and let them rest for 1 hour.
- Shape into mini burgers and fry over medium heat till golden brown.
- Serve with extra onions fried separately, hamburger bread, or brown bread. Lovely also as cocktail burgers with a good chutney or dip.

Serves 4 – 6

. . . .

Adil's succulent roast chicken

Get two plump farm chickens, roast them as I instruct, eat one hot; the other one can be eaten the following day cold in a salad or in yummy sandwiches. I brine it for 3 hours ... this tenderises the chicken and renders it very moist ... try.

Ingredients

- 2 roast chickens, gizzards removed. (Place in a deep basin filled with water)
- 4 tbsp salt (stir well). Let the chicken sit in this for at least 3 hours. Remove, part dry outside and in.
  In the cavity of both chickens add:
- Some salt and pepper
- 2 cut lemons
- some whole cloves of garlic
- mixed herbs
- some sliced onions

Method

- Place in a baking tray, massage plenty of oil, then season with salt and pepper, around the tray, add some more garlic, onions halved, rosemary, sage, and leek.
- Cover with foil and bake at 200°C for twenty minutes, reduce the temperature to 190°C and let cook for another 1 hour and 15 minutes.
- Switch off the oven and leave the door slightly ajar. Let the chicken rest for about 25 minutes.
- After this, carve and serve with vegetables, salads, sautéed potatoes. You can make gravy too by using the juices left in the tray (drain oil) add about 2 tsp of corn flour stirring all the time, over medium heat.
- Season well. The chicken is so lovely that I am sure you will try this recipe again and again ... thinking of me!

Serves 4

. . . .

Picnic spring chicken . . . kuku kweli kweli

Our version of chicken on the go. If you cannot get spring chickens use normal ones ¼ed.

Ingredients

- 2 spring chickens halved and mixed in a paste of:
- 2 tsp salt
- 1 tsp mild paprika
- 2 tsp red pepper
- 1 tsp freshly milled black pepper
- 2 tsp ground cumin
- 2 tsp ginger crushed
- 2 tsp garlic crushed
- 4 tbsp oil
- 3 tbsp thick yoghurt

Method

- Let the chicken marinate in this for at least 6 hours or overnight.
- Next day bring it to room temperature, bake in a tray covered with foil for an hour at 200°C, uncover and bake further till golden brown and cooked through.
- Eat with fresh warmed pitta bread and crispy salad, topped with garlic mayo … just add the required amount of garlic to the mayonnaise, season well, add some lemon juice and hey, you are in heaven!!

Serves 4

. . . .

Poached chicken . . .

Poached chicken, a real money saver, you can use the fresh stock for soup and the chicken in sandwiches or a salad (like a potato salad with chicken etc).

Ingredients

In a large pot add:
- 1 plump chicken
- 6 carrots peeled
- bay leaf
- 6 cloves garlic
- 10 whole peppercorns
- 4 sticks celery cleaned
- 4 leeks cleaned well
- 3 stock cubes (chicken or vegetables)
- ½ a bottle of white wine
- enough water to cover chicken

Method

- Bring to boil, skim every now and then, lower heat to the absolute low and let it cook till the chicken is tender. This can take about 2 hours, depending on how plump your chicken is.
- Do not overcook. This recipe again leaves lots of time to attend to other things. Serve with mayo that you may flavour with curry powder, or garlic.
- Even the vegetables can be eaten … just season and dribble some olive oil.

Serves 4

. . . .

Chicken satay kebabs

These kebabs need marination overnight to develop their full flavour, utterly delicious, well worth the wait …

Ingredients

- 4 large skinless chicken breasts, cut into large cubes
  The sauce:
- 4 small onions grated
- 3 cloves of garlic crushed
- 3 tsp fresh ginger pounded
- 3 tbsp brown sugar
- 3 tbsp light soya sauce
- 2 tsp mixed spice
- 4 tsp peanut butter
- 1 tsp fish sauce (optional)
- 2 tbsp oil
- 1 green chilli chopped (more if you like a kick)
- juice of 3 limes
- salt and pepper

Method

- In a bowl, mix the sauce ingredients first, check the seasoning, including the sugar level, place the chicken cubes into it, cover and place in the refrigerator, leave overnight.
- Remove from the fridge half an hour before using.
- Place on skewers and grill on a barbie or electric grill, turning till nicely browned (6 minutes or so).
- Serve with a green salad, dressed and warmed buttered pitta bread.

Serves 4

. . . .

Paprika chicken with saffron dumplings

A warming dish that comforts you on a cold day. Use smoked paprika for a authentic taste.

Ingredients

- 1 tbsp oil
- 10 chicken breasts
- 2 stalks celery chopped
- 2 carrots peeled and cut into rings
- 1 medium onion chopped
- 2 cloves garlic crushed
- 3 tbsp paprika
- salt and pepper to taste
- 2 cans chicken stock or 2 stock cubes with the equivalent liquid (about 4 cups warm water)
- 1 cup white wine
- parsley for garnish
  Dumplings ...
- ½ cup warm milk mixed with ½ tsp saffron
- 1 cup all purpose flour (baking flour)
- 1½ tsp baking powder
- 2 tbsp margarine (use the good kind with no hydrogenated oil)
- ½ cup parsley

Method

- For the dumplings, mix all the ingredients together, cover and let rest for 20 minutes.

For the chicken ...

- In a large pan that has a lid, add the oil on a medium flame, brown the chicken, add all the ingredients except the liquid (stock and wine).
- Sauté for 4 minutes, add the stock and the wine bring to boil, let the alcohol evaporate (about 4 minutes).
- Lower heat to a simmer, cook for 20 minutes or so, make little golfballs with the dumplings, add to the chicken mix, cover and let simmer for 15 minutes, try not to peek till then.
- When the dumplings float they are done.
- Garnish with parsley.
- Serve with some warm French bread to help soak up the juices.

Serves 6 – 8

. . . .

Kenya sunset chicken

A dish that reflects upon our spectacular sunsets and tastes ...

Ingredients

- a little yoghurt and garlic mixed
- 6 chicken breasts cubed
- 130 gm butter
- 800 ml fresh orange juice
- rinds of 3 oranges grated finely (avoid pesticide oranges)
- some rosemary
- 1 cup cashews chopped
- 1 tsp cointreau
- season well with salt and pepper

Method

- Add the yoghurt to the chicken and let marinate for a while (2 hours if possible) rinse well and dry.
- Stir fry chicken, for a while till browned.
- Add the orange rind, rosemary, orange juice, put the heat on high and reduce the liquid, adding the cointreau – and cashews.
- Season well. Serve with rice, ugali, (polenta) or plain potatoes.
- For an extra kick, add some Tabasco.

Serves 6

. . . .

Chicken liver paté

Ingredients

- 1 kg (22 lb) chicken livers, cleaned
- 2 finely chopped onions
- 4 cloves garlic, crushed
- ½ wine glass dry sherry
- 1 wine glass brandy
- 4 tbsp butter
- ½ tsp mixed herbs
- 2 bay leaves
- salt and pepper to taste

Method

- Over medium heat, melt the butter and fry the onions and chicken livers for about 5 minutes. Add the sherry, brandy, garlic, herbs, bay leaf and seasoning.

- Let the mixture cool a little.
- Remove the bay leaf and liquidize until the required consistency is achieved.
- Pour into a baking dish, add a knob of butter and bake in a moderate oven for about 7 minutes.
- Cool and refrigerate. The paté will keep in the refrigerator for up to 1½ weeks. If in doubt, the smell will tell you whether it is still fresh.

Hint: Some chicken stock may be added while you liquidize.

Serves 4

. . . .

Chicken tikka . . . the Kenyan way

Ingredients

- 2 chicken, cut up and scored
- 2 cups onions, finely sliced
- 6 – 8 cloves garlic, crushed
- 3 tbsp ginger, crushed
- 2 bunches fresh dhania, chopped
- 3 cups plain yoghurt
- ½ cup cream
- 6 tbsp lime juice
- ¼ cup oil
- 3 tbsp coriander power
- 3 tbsp cumin power
- 1 tbsp garam masala
- 2 cardamoms, crushed
- ½ tsp red chilli powder
- 1 tbsp salt

Method

- Mix all the ingredients together and marinate for at least 12 hours in the refrigerator, turning the chicken pieces from time to time.
- Before cooking, allow the ingredients to return to room temperature. Pre-heat the oven to medium.
- Generously grease a baking dish using butter and place the chicken in it.
- Put in the oven and allow to roast for about 1 hour 20 minutes, turning the pieces every half hour.
- Serve with salad, warm bread and mint sauce.

Hint: A ready-made garam masala mix is available at supermarkets – but even the infamous curry powder produces good results.

Serves 6

Chicken wings

There are so many ways to prepare chicken wings. But once you try this recipe, you will never want them any other way!

Ingredients

- 1 kg (22 lb) chicken wings, scored on the fleshy part
- 6 tbsp soya sauce
- 3 tsp sweet sherry or port
- 1½ tbsp corn flour
- 2 onions, roughly chopped
- 8 cloves garlic, crushed
- 1 cup vegetable oil
- 1½ cups lime juice
- cayenne pepper to taste
- salt and freshly milled pepper to taste

Method

- Mix the corn flour, soya sauce and lime juice.
- Add the rest of the ingredients and mix well.
- Marinate for 12 hours in the refrigerator.
- Remove from the refrigerator and allow to sit until it gets to room temperature.
- Grill over a medium fire for about 12 minutes each side, basting every 4 minutes.

Serves 4

. . . .

Coq au vin

Simply a stew with a fancy name.

Ingredients

- 1 medium chicken, cut up
- 10 rashers beef bacon, trimmed and chopped
- ½ punnet mushrooms, sliced (optional)
- 20 button onions, whole or 2 onions, chopped
- 4 cloves garlic, crushed
- 4 tbsp butter
- 2 chicken stock cubes,
- ½ wine glass brandy
- ¾ bottle reasonable red wine
- ½ (17.5 fl oz) water
- corn flour (optional)
- 1 tsp mixed herbs
- salt and freshly milled pepper to taste, and parsley

Method

- Brown the chicken slowly and evenly in the butter.
- Put in the onions and bacon, pour in the wine, add the garlic, herbs, stock cubes, water, seasoning and button mushrooms if liked.
- Cook slowly on low heat for about an hour. If it needs thickening, add one tsp of corn flour mixed with a little water.
- Flame with brandy and add parsley.
- Serve with creamed potatoes or rice, accompanied with warm bread to mop up the sauce.

Serves 4

....

Chicken tarragon

"Kuku" with a difference.

Ingredients

- 1 roasting chicken
- 1 cup mushrooms, chopped
- 1 bunch spring onions, washed well and chopped
- 1 cup cream cheese
- ½ cup breadcrumbs
- 3 tbsp butter
- 1 stock cube dissolved in one cup of warm water
- 1 tbsp olive oil
- 2 tbsp fresh tarragon, chopped (or 1 tbsp dry tarragon)
- ½ bunch chopped parsley
- salt and freshly milled pepper to taste
- silver foil

Method

- Pre-heat oven to 250°C (gas mark 7).
- Mix all the herbs, mushrooms, breadcrumbs and spring onions well with the cream cheese and butter. Loosely fill the cavity of the chicken with this mixture, leaving some to "smear" over the chicken.
- Mix the stock with the olive oil.
- Place the chicken onto a baking tray and pour the stock mixture over and around it. Sprinkle with salt and pepper. Cover the baking tray tightly with foil and place in the oven.
- After 20 minutes reduce the oven temperature to 200°C (gas mark 6) and continue to roast for 40 minutes.
- Remove the foil, baste the chicken well and return it to the oven for a further half hour, allowing it to brown well. The skin should become crisp.

Serves 4

Chicken with cream

I have often admired the taste of this excellent dish.

Ingredients

- 1 chicken, cut into pieces
- 5 tbsp butter
- 2 glasses dry white wine
- 1 cup double cream
- ½ tsp corn flour
- 1 stock cube dissolved in 400 ml (15 fl oz) water
- salt and freshly milled pepper
- parsley to garnish

Method

- Heat 4 tbsp of the butter in a cast iron pan over a medium flame.
- Add the chicken, starting with the drumsticks followed by the other pieces after a few minutes.
- Do not allow the chicken to brown.
- Add the stock and cover. Lower heat and allow to cook for about 45 minutes
- Check the liquid level and add a little water if necessary.
- When the chicken is cooked, adjust the flame to high and add the wine. It should evaporate quickly (you can smell it evaporating).
- Lower the heat, add the cream slowly and allow to simmer for 5 minutes.
- Add salt and pepper according to taste with the remaining butter and turn into a serving dish.
- Garnish with parsley.
- Serve with rice, new potatoes or creamed potatoes.

Serves 4

. . . .

Roast chicken

Sometimes – more often than not, simple things are the best.

Ingredients

- 1 chicken weighing about 1 kg (2.2 lb)
- 3 tbsp oil
  For the stuffing:
- 1 egg
- 2 slices of bread
- 1 tbsp butter
- 1 onion, chopped
- ¾ tsp mixed herbs
- a small sprig of rosemary
- 1 tbsp mushrooms, finely chopped

- 2 tbsp cream
- olive oil or salad oil
- salt and pepper

Method

- Pre-heat the oven to high (250°C).
- Mix the stuffing ingredients well.
- Stuff the chicken without over-packing and set onto a tray.
- Lightly brush the chicken with oil, adding a little to the baking tray with a cup of water.
- Put the chicken in the oven, lowering the heat after 15 minutes to about 200°C.
- Baste often, and do not allow the water in the baking tray to dry out. After about an hour and 15 minutes it should be ready.
- Use the liquid remaining in the baking tray as gravy.
- Serve with sauté potatoes, vegetables of your choice and a salad.

Hint: Alternatively you can stuff the chicken with mixed herbs, 1 cup of fresh breadcrumbs, an egg, ¾ tsp rosemary and 10 cloves of garlic with seasoning for a very tasty roast chicken.

Serves 4

· · · · · · · · · · · · · · · · · · · ·

Chicken hollandaise

So heavenly!

Ingredients

- 5 chicken breasts
- 1 egg, beaten
- breadcrumbs, lightly seasoned
- salad oil (enough to cover the bottom of the pan)
- parsley to garnish
  For the sauce:
- 2 egg yolks, beaten
- 125 gm (4 oz) butter, melted
- 4 tbsp dry white wine
- 2 tbsp lime juice
- salt and freshly milled pepper

Method

- Coat the chicken breasts with the beaten egg and then roll in the breadcrumbs.
- Fry over a medium flame until brown and cooked through.
- Put it aside and keep it warm in a medium oven.

- For the sauce: never heat this sauce violently as it will curdle. If this happens, add a little hot water, stirring. It may come back.
- Heat the wine in a pan until it reduces by half. Place it aside.
- Place the egg yolks in a bain-marie or double boiler and whisk energetically.
- Add the wine gradually. Still stirring rapidly, add the butter very slowly. The sauce will start to thicken.
- Remove from heat and add lime juice and seasoning.
- Pour the sauce over the chicken breasts, garnish and serve immediately.

Hint: If the sauce curdles, add a little hot water drop by drop, while stirring constantly.

Serves 5 – 6

· · · · · · · · · · · · · · · · · · · ·

Chicken livers

To me, this dish is as addictive as chocolate.

Ingredients

- 500 gm (1 lb) chicken livers, cleaned
- 8 tbsp oil
- 3 tbsp soya sauce
- 2 tbsp ginger, crushed
- 8 tbsp dry sherry
- 200 gm (7 oz) snow-peas, blanched
- ½ tsp sugar
- 1½ tsp salt
- ½ cup water
- ½ bunch spring onions, finely chopped, to garnish

Method

- Heat the oil over a high flame and add the chicken livers.
- Fry for about 3 minutes, stirring all the time.
- Add the sherry followed by the ginger, soya sauce, sugar and salt.
- Lower heat, add water and snow-peas and allow it to simmer for a few minutes. Normally the liver should be pale pink inside. If you like your liver well done, increase the heat for the last few minutes before serving.
- Top with spring onions. Serve with noodles or rice.

Hint: To avoid overcooking the snow-peas, add them to the liver 5 minutes before removing the pan from the fire.

Serves 4

· · · · · · · · · · · · · · · · · · · ·

Chicken livers with cream and nuts
Even more addictive!

Ingredients

- 500 gm (16 oz) chicken livers, cleaned
- 5 onions, finely chopped
- 2 cups cream mixed with 1 tsp corn flour
- ½ cup brandy
- ½ cup vegetable oil
- salt and freshly milled pepper
  To garnish:
- parsley
- spring onions
- ¼ cup pine nuts or almonds, blanched and crushed

Method

- Sauté the onions in the oil until they turn light brown.
- Add the chicken and cook for 5 minutes or longer if you want them completely cooked. Lower heat and add the cream.
- Flame the brandy if you can or just add it and simmer for a few minutes. Meanwhile, have a warm serving dish ready.
- Remove the liver from the fire. Pour it into the warmed serving dish and garnish with the parsley, nuts and spring onions.
- Serve with noodles and a salad of your choice.

Hint: The easiest way of flaming is to warm the brandy in a large spoon or pan, add it swiftly to the ingredients and light it either by tilting the pan towards the gas flame or, if you are using an electric cooker, use a cigarette lighter. But remember to keep your head clear, otherwise you might end up with singed hair or eyebrows!

Serves 4

. . . .

Jeera chicken
A delicate cumin curry.

Ingredients

- 1 chicken, portioned
- 2 onions, finely sliced
- 3 tomatoes, peeled and finely chopped
- 4 cloves garlic, crushed
- 1 tbsp ginger, crushed
- 1 stock cube dissolved in 2 cups hot water
- 2½ tbsp crushed cumin seeds
- green chillies according to your taste

- a sprinkling of dhania
- 4 tbsp butter
- 1 tbsp corn oil
- salt and freshly milled pepper

Method

- Put the butter and vegetable oil in a pan and fry the onions until they are clear.
- Add the cumin seeds and the chicken and continue to fry over a medium flame until the chicken is lightly browned.
- Add the tomatoes, garlic and ginger.
- Simmer for 10 minutes, and then pour in the stock.
- Simmer for a further 40 minutes, constantly checking that the liquid does not dry out.
- Add the green chillies with the rest of the seasoning ingredients and sprinkle with dhania.
- Serve with rice.

To vary the recipe:

- A slightly different version of this dish can be created by adding 1 cup of yoghurt mixed with ¾ tsp corn flour to the chicken towards the end of cooking.
- Allow this to simmer for 5 minutes and add 1 tsp of garam masala before serving.

Serves 4

....

Chicken and seafood gumbo

A delectable Creole dish.

Ingredients

- 1 chicken, cut up
- 220 gm (7 oz) prawns, peeled, de-veined and washed
- 2 lobster tails with flesh removed
- 1 tin mussels (optional)
- 750 gm (24 oz) okra (ladies' fingers), whole if small; cut in ½ if large
- 125 gm (4 oz) carrots, diced
- 4 onions, sliced
- 4 cloves garlic, crushed
- 155 gm (5 oz) spring onions, finely chopped
- 6 tomatoes, peeled and chopped
- 90 gms (3 oz) celery, chopped
- 2 tbsp butter
- 4 tbsp oil
- 2 stock cubes dissolved in 4 cups hot water

- juice of 1 lime
- a dash of tabasco
- ¼ tsp thyme
- ½ a bunch parsley, chopped
- ¼ tsp basil
- salt and freshly milled pepper

Method

- Trim the okra and blanch in hot, salted water. Drain and put aside. In a heavy pan, mix the butter with the oil, heat it and sauté the onions.
- Put the chicken in the pan and brown it slightly. Add the carrots, celery, tomatoes, garlic and lime juice.
- Lower the heat and add the stock.
- Allow it to simmer for 10 minutes.
- Add the okra, prawns, lobster and mussels and simmer for 20 minutes.
- Add seasoning, herbs and spring onions, allowing it to simmer for 5 more minutes.
- Turn into a serving dish.

Serves 6

· · · · · · · · · · · · · · · · · · · ·

Deep-fried chicken

Another version for you.

Ingredients

- 1 chicken, cut up
- 1 carrot, chopped
- 1 onion, chopped
- 4 cloves garlic, crushed
- 1 stick celery, chopped
- 2 tbsp ginger, crushed
- 1 stock cube
- ½ tsp mixed herbs
- 1 tsp butter
- salt and freshly milled pepper
  For the coating:
- 2 cups breadcrumbs, seasoned
- 2 eggs, beaten
- oil for frying

Method

- Boil some water in a large pan and put in all the ingredients.
- Cover and simmer for about 20 minutes.
- Remove the chicken using a slotted spoon and allow it to cool.

- Coat the chicken pieces with egg and then roll them in the breadcrumbs. Do this twice.
- Heat the oil in a deep frying pan over a medium flame.
- Place the chicken pieces in the oil, beginning with the drumsticks, followed by the thighs and then the rest of the pieces. Fry until golden brown.
- Remember, the chicken is already half cooked so it will not take long to be done.

Hint: Do not discard the chicken stock water. It can be frozen for use later. Use it to make spicy soups and casseroles.

Serves 4

. . . .

Chapter 4

Beef

Marinated coastal kebabs

These little gems need to sleep overnight in the marinade, once put on skewers and grilled; all you need is a few simple dips and chutneys topped by a crisp salad. Indeed you could put them in warmed buttery pitta bread, alongside some salad, tomatoes and cucumber. Remember to season well … a good dollop of thick yoghurt will hit the spot right on.

Ingredients

In a large bowl, mix:
- 4 cloves garlic crushed
- 3 tbsp ginger crushed
- 1 large onion grated
- 3 tbsp honey
- 1 tbsp soy sauce
- 1 green chilli finely chopped
- zest of 1 lemon (not the pith and make sure there are no insecticides . . . use organic)
- 2 tbsp Worcestershire sauce
- ½ tsp freshly ground pepper
- salt to be added at the end of cooking
- 800 gm beef fillet, cut into cubes (about 4 cm long and 2 cm thick) and lightly flattened

Method
- Mix well and place in the refrigerator overnight.
- Remove an hour before use.
- Place on skewers and grill about 4 minutes each side, basting with the left marinade as you go along.
- The yoghurt that you use may be flavoured with some fresh garlic and seasoned with salt and pepper or with roasted cumin, red chilli and salt. A meal that comforts as you eat and is sinfully satisfying.

Serves 4 – 6

. . . .

Molo highland beef steaks

Soft, tender and flavoursome, these steaks also need marinating overnight for maximum effect, so do not rush. Try to cook them no more than medium rare or they will toughen up a bit. Use the best quality beef for melt in the mouth results!

Ingredients

- 4 prime fillet steaks, beaten lightly with a wooden hammer or rolling pin.
  Add these to the following marinade:
- 3 cloves garlic crushed
- 1 tbsp ginger crushed
- 1 tsp red wine vinegar
- 1 tbsp sesame oil
- 1 tsp olive oil
- 3 spring onions finely chopped
- 3 tbsp dry sherry
- 3 tbsp dark soy sauce
- 1 tbsp sweet chilli sauce
- 1 tbsp sugar
- ½ tsp freshly ground pepper

Method

- Place the mixture in the refrigerator till the next day.
- Remove an hour before use.
- Heat your griddle pan or frying pan till very hot, add the steaks and sear for 3 minutes each side (may be 4 if you want it done med rare). Keep warm and serve with baked potatoes that have cream cheese and chives in them, French fries or mashed potatoes and a mixed salad.
- The key to success is not to overcook the meat and to let it rest a few moments before serving.

Serves 4

. . . .

Meat loaf

When I first heard about meat loaf, I was a little dismayed to think of a block of mince being baked in an oven like a cake and eaten hot or cold. But there is something to be said of meat loaf and I hope that here in Kenya the trend picks up. It is portable ... good for picnics, children's break or lunch and is a way of stretching the week a bit like sukuma wiki. Kids love it on bread (use wholemeal) with plenty of mayonnaise and salad . . . try it.

Ingredients

- 1 cup onions finely diced and fried lightly till clear. *Cool and add to the rest . . .*
- 2.2 kg beef mince (can be ½ beef and ½ pork)
- 1 egg beaten
- 2 tbsp chopped parsley
- 3 cloves garlic crushed
- 1 tsp salt
- ½ tsp freshly ground pepper
- ½ cup good tomato ketchup
- ¼ tsp thyme
- ¼ tsp sage
- ¼ tsp nutmeg
- ¼ tsp freshly milled pepper
- ½ tsp paprika
- ¼ cup cream
- 2 tbsp fresh bread crumbs (simply grate fresh or day old bread)
- 1 tsp lime juice
- a dash of tabasco

Method

- Mix all the ingredients very well.
- Place in a greased bread loaf tin, dot the two with lashings of butter.
- Cover and bake at 180°C for 45 minutes uncover and bake for 20 minutes or till browned.

Serves 6 – 8

. . . .

Beef strips with ginger and chilli

Sure to please everyone.

Ingredients

- 600 gm beef fillet finely sliced
- 3 tbsp oyster sauce
- 1 tsp sesame oil
- 4 tbsp light soya sauce
- ½ tsp sugar
- salt and freshly milled pepper
- oil for stir frying (about ¼ cup)
- 6 cloves garlic crushed
- 3 tsp grated ginger
- a good hand full of sugar, peas, diced carrots, and water chestnuts (optional)
- 4 – 5 minced green chillies

Method

- In a bowl mix the beef, oyster sauce, soya sauce, sesame oil and seasoning.
- Leave to marinate at least an hour. In a large pan, heat the oil to smoking point, flash fry the garlic, ginger, add the meat stirring fast. followed by vegetables, then the chillies. If too thick add a little water.
- Check seasoning.
- Serve with noodles, or fragrant Thai rice.

Serves 4

. . . .

Minute steak with onions

An easy quick recipe, served with good bread of your choice, golden onions and a salad. One hour marinating is needed, so start early.

Ingredients

- 500 gm fillet steak (sliced)
- extra oil for stir frying the meat and onions
  Marinade:
- 6 tbsp red wine
- 3 tbsp soy sauce
- 1 tbsp mustard of your choice
- 1 tbsp Worcestershire sauce
- 1 clove garlic minced

Method

- Place the steak slices in the marinade above and mix well. Let this sit for about 1 hour.
- Meanwhile slice 2 onions and fry them on high heat till golden brown.
- Set aside … keep warm.
- On a high heat place a heavy pan with oil and when smoking, add the steak. 2 – 3 minutes a side should do it, unless you intend to eat fresh leather!
- Toast the bread, smother it with garlic mayonnaise, lay the steak on, topped with the onions. A dish truly made for Kenya.

Serves 4

. . . .

Quick hamburgers

This is a very versatile recipe for those hungry impatient kids. Much better than those dreadful ones we get trapped to buy.

Ingredients

- 700 gm mince meat
- ½ a cup breadcrumbs
- ½ a cup parmesan or romano cheese, grated
- 2 onions sliced thinly, lightly fried till clear, cooled and added
- 1 egg
- ½ a cup readymade tomato sauce (available as a pasta base sauce in supermarkets. Omit if not available and add 1 tbsp tomato puree)
- 1 tbsp basil
- 1 tbsp parsley
- 1 clove garlic crushed
- good dash lea and perrins (Worcestershire sauce)
- salt and pepper

Method

- Mix the above ingredients well, and let rest for 30 minutes before using.
- With damp hands shape into balls, then flatten as hamburgers.
- Place in a pan or under a grill lightly greased and cook for 4 minutes each side or till they are done to your liking.
- Serve with warmed hamburger bread or whatever kind of bread you like, alongside lots of lettuce, onion rings, ketchup, gherkins and cheese slices.
- Compared to the ones we buy these are famously wicked.

Serves 4

. . . .

Zesty orange beef kebabs

These cubes of meat need to marinate 24 hours in the refrigerator, do remove them half an hour before use. Serve alongside some mayonnaise with crushed garlic added to it and a green salad. Lovely too in pitta bread pockets with coleslaw.

Ingredients

- 1 kg prime filleted cut into cubes
  The marinade...
- 2 tsp cointreau (orange liquor . . . or the equivalent)
- 1 tbsp brown sugar
- 5 tbsp soya sauce
- 4 cloves garlic crushed
- 2 tsp ginger pounded
- 2 tsp ground cumin
- 1 tsp ground coriander

- ½ tsp black pepper
- 2 tsp Worcestershire sauce
- 2 tbsp lime juice
- 1 tsp orange zest grated ... do not use the white pith
- 3 tbsp olive oil

Method

- Place the meat in the marinade and let it sit in the refrigerator for 24 hours.
- Thread onto skewers and grill, basting with a little of the marinade as you go along. For peeks sake, do not overcook.
- Serve as mentioned above, or make quick chutney using yoghurt, with lots of dhania and a couple of green chillies whizzed in a food processor.
- Season with salt. You may use chicken breast as variation or even split the marinade in half and do both!

Serves 4 – 6

. . . .

Steak with a piquant sauce

A truly Kenyan recipe with a touch of Italian.

Ingredients

- 750 gm steak sliced
  The sauce:
- 6 tbsp good olive oil
- 4 onions thinly sliced
- 4 cloves garlic crushed
- 4 tsp freshly grated ginger
- 750 gm tomatoes chopped finely
- 1 tbsp tomato puree
- ½ a cup red wine
- salt and pepper to taste, a good pinch sugar and several dashes hot sauce
- some chopped fresh coriander to garnish
- extra oil with a knob of butter for the steak

Method

- First make the sauce by adding the olive oil to a pan on medium heat.
- Place the onions in the pan and sauté till clear; add the ginger and garlic, followed by the tomatoes and the puree after one minute.
- When the tomatoes brake down (add a little water if it gets too dry) add the wine and simmer ... season with the salt, pepper, sugar and hot sauce.
- Stir well and taste to check the seasoning. Keep warm. For the steak, simply pan fry using the oil and butter mixture.

- Try not to overcook even if you like it well done. Ideally you should fry them no more than about 3 minutes per side, although this varies with the thickness of the meat.
- Place the steaks on a warmed platter, top with the reheated sauce and garnish with chopped coriander. This dish can be enjoyed with our *sukuma wiki* (local spinach) mashed potatoes and, or coleslaw. Utterly exquisite.

Serve 4

....

Chilli honey grilled shrimp

Done at home it is cheaper, tastier and will win you a lot of compliments, go for it!

Ingredients

- 1 kg large shrimp, deveined
- ½ cup lime juice
- ½ cup hoi sin sauce
- ½ cup honey
- a tsp chilli sauce
- 2 tbsp sesame seeds
- 4 cloves garlic minced
- 2 tsp freshly grated ginger

Method

- Mix all the above ingredients well. Marinade for at least an hour in a cool place. When ready to eat, turn the grill to medium high, place shrimp on the rack and grill each side for about 2 minutes.
- Baste well at least twice.
- Serve with a rich garlic mayonnaise (simply add crushed garlic to seasoned mayonnaise ... the amount of garlic added is up to you, though a slightly strong flavour is better in this case). A fair indication that the shrimp is cooked through is when it turns pink.

Serves 4

....

Beef kebabs

This needs overnight marinating so start one day in advance.

Ingredients

- I kg steak, cubed
  The Marinade is as follows:
- juice of 1 lime
- ½ tsp salt
- 1 tsp cumin powder

- 2 cups yoghurt
- 1 onion grated
- 1 tsp garam masala
- 3 cloves garlic crushed
- 1 tbsp ginger finely chopped or crushed
- 1 tsp paprika powder (optional)
- 1 green chilli chopped
- handful of fresh coriander chopped
- extra oil for basting

Method

- Mix the ingredients of the marinade well; add the cubed meat, coating it.
- Refrigerate overnight and remove an hour before grilling.
- Thread the meat on skewers and grill on a medium heat, till done to your liking, basting with the extra oil as needed.
- Serve with warm nan bread, a green salad, or a traditional *kachumbari*. (Thin slices of tomatoes, onions, cucumber, seasoned with salt, red chilli, a dash of malt vinegar). You may add some green peppers on the skewers or onions etc.
- Another good idea is to buy pitta bread, warm it up, make a pocket by slitting the side and stuffing it with the meat combined with some coleslaw. Better than any fast food available by miles.

Serves 4 – 6 depending on appetite!

. . . .

Louisiana style steaks

A magic mix of herbs spices that needs marinating so start a day ahead.

Ingredients

- 1 kg of prime fillet, cut into steaks and mildly beaten with a mallet
- 1 onion grated
- 2 cloves garlic crushed
- 2 tsp ginger pounded
- ½ cup oil (or a little more)
- 1 tsp cumin
- 1 tsp paprika (smoked if you have it)
- 1 tsp cayenne pepper
- 1 tsp black pepper
- 1 tsp onion powder
- 1 tsp chilli powder
- 1 tsp dried thyme
- 1 tsp dried basil
- 1 tsp dried oregano

Method

- Mix all the above well together and place in a bowl, cover and refrigerate for 24 hours.
- Remove well ½ an hour before you intend to cook it. If the steaks are 'wet' wipe clean with kitchen paper.
- In a pan add some additional oil and a little butter, add the steaks till done to your liking.
- Do not prod it all the time and if you must check by cutting, just take a little from the side off.
- You can serve this with French fries, mash, vegetables of your choice, or simply in a warm baguette, dripping with butter!

Serves 4

....

Shish kebabs

A nice nyama choma (BBQ) dish. Needs time for marination.

Ingredients

- 1 kg steak, lightly beaten
- ½ cup yoghurt
- 2 onions crushed
- 2 green chilli minced
- 1 tsp cumin seeds
- ½ tsp black pepper
- 1 tbsp crushed ginger
- 1 tbsp crushed garlic
- 1 tbsp tomato puree
- juice of 1 lime
- 2 tbsp oil
- 1 tsp salt.
- extra oil for coating the meat whilst you BBQ

Method

- Mix all the ingredients well (except the extra oil). Let this marinate for at least 6 hours or overnight in the fridge.
- Remove at least 1 hour before needed. Place the meat on skewers and BBQ, coating as needed. You can use an electric grill but the flavour will be somewhat inferior.
- Serve with some cool yoghurt, sprinkled with some dry roasted cumin seeds and fresh coriander, season with pepper and red chilli.
- Eat with nan bread, a salad, or place in hamburger buns with some salad and lots of dripping butter or mayo. Mmmmm!

Serves 4 – 6

Spicy Nakuru hamburgers

My home town, small, cute and beautiful. Quite a delight, the secret is in frying the onions first, letting them cool and adding to the meat with fresh coriander. Place in a bun dripping with butter and the result is ecstasy.

Ingredients

- 1 kg of mince meat (ground meat) of your choice
- 2 onions fried till clear and added when cool to the meat
  The rest of the ingredients just need to be added to the mince:
- 2 tsp crushed garlic
- 2 tsp ground ginger (fresh)
- 2 tsp salt
- 2 tsp cumin seeds
- 1 tsp fenugreek seeds (crushed) or leaves … optional as the taste is acquired
- 2 green chillies finely chopped or as hot as you like
- 1 tsp garam masala
- 1 egg beaten
- ½ cup breadcrumbs

Method

- Mix well and let rest for 20 minutes.
- Form into hamburgers. If the meat gets too sticky, simply wash your hands and keep them wet … it works, and fry in a little oil untill cooked to your liking.
- Serve in warmed buns, with a nice salad, or unhealthy French fries! Top with cheese and we have Kenyan MacDonald's!

Serves 4 – 6

. . . .

Norwegian meat balls

Ingredients

- ½ kg beef mince
- ½ kg pork mince
- 5 slices stale bread soaked in ½ cup milk
- 1 tsp salt
- ½ tsp black pepper
- 1 tsp nutmeg
- 1 onion thinly sliced (lightly fried in advance till clear)
- 1 tbsp tomato puree

- 1 cup chicken stock (use 1 stock cube in hot water)
- extra flour for coating the meat balls
- oil for light frying

Method

- Mix all the ingredients in a bowl **except** the tomato puree and flour.
- Roll the mix into balls.
- Coat evenly with the flour.
- Fry in a pan with the oil and brown well, add the stock and the tomato puree.
- Season with added salt and pepper if needed. Serve with boiled potatoes, brussels
sprouts and or cabbage. A Norwegian recipe that adapts so well in Kenya.

Serves 4 – 6

. . . .

Steak diane

Ingredients *ariations to this recipe. This one will keep you on your toes.*

- 4 slices of fillet steak
- ½ cup red wine
- ½ tsp mixed herbs
- 3 tomatoes, skinned and chopped
- 3 onions, finely chopped
- 2 cloves garlic, crushed (optional)
- 1 cup mushrooms, washed, soaked in water with a little vinegar, sliced
- 4 tbsp butter
- 2 tbsp oil
- a dash of Worcestershire sauce
- a dash of tabasco
- 3 tbsp brandy
- ½ cup cream mixed with ½ tsp corn flour
- salt and freshly milled pepper to taste
- 1 tsp paté (optional)
- parsley to garnish

Method

- Beat the steak with a mallet and marinate it in the red wine and mixed herbs for about 4 hours at room temperature.
- Pre-heat the oven to medium heat.
- Reserving the marinade, fry the steak in a heavy-based pan with the butter and oil until it is almost done to your liking.

- Place in a casserole and put it in the oven. Lower heat.
- Meanwhile, sauté the onions in the fat used to fry the steak and add the garlic if liked, then the tomatoes followed by the mushrooms.
- Add Worcestershire and tabasco sauce and season.
- Add the cream and simmer. Do not allow to boil. If the mixture is too thick, add a little of the reserved marinating liquid. Stir in the brandy and flame, keeping your eyelashes well out of the way! By this time the steaks should be done to your liking.
- Remove from the oven and pour the mushroom sauce over the steaks.
- Top with a little paté, if liked, and parsley.

Serves 4

. . . .

Beef with rosemary

This is an easy, tasty dish.

Ingredients

- 1 kg (2.2 lb) stewing beef or rump steak, cubed
- 4 onions, finely sliced
- 6 tomatoes, skinned and sliced
- 4 cloves garlic, crushed
- 1 tsp fresh ginger, crushed
- 2 stock cubes dissolved in one cup hot water
- 3 cups dry red wine
- 1 tsp fresh rosemary
- ½ cup cream mixed with ½ tsp corn flour
- 4 tbsp butter
- a little water
- salt and freshly milled pepper to taste

Method

- Pre-heat the oven to 200°C (gas mark 3).
- Melt the butter in a pan and add the onions and meat, over a medium flame, until lightly browned.
- Add the tomatoes, garlic, ginger and rosemary.
- Simmer for a few minutes, and then turn these ingredients into a casserole dish, add the wine and season with salt and pepper.
- Place in the pre-heated oven for about 2 hours.
- Check the liquid content and add water if needed. When the meat is tender, add the cream, mix well and return to the oven for a further 10 minutes.
- Serve with rice or noodles and vegetables of your choice. Or, if you intend to have a lazy day, serve with creamed potatoes and a green salad.

Serves 4

Beef saté with green pepper

Ingredients

- 1 kg (2.2 lb) stewing steak, cubed
- ½ kg. (1.1 lb) peanuts, shelled, roasted and ground in a coffee grinder or a food processor
- 4 onions, thinly sliced
- 4 tomatoes, skinned and sliced
- 1 tbsp tomato purée
- 4 cloves garlic, crushed
- 2 tsp ginger, crushed
- 2 green peppers, seeded, sliced and blanched in hot water for 1 minute
- ½ cup oil
- juice of 1 lime
- 1 stock cube dissolved in ½ l (17.5 fl oz) hot water
- 2 tbsp peanut butter (optional)
- cayenne pepper
- dhania
- salt and freshly milled pepper

Method

- Fry the onions in the oil until almost golden.
- Add meat and tomatoes and continue frying until the tomatoes are tender.
- Add garlic, ginger, tomato purée and stock.
- Reduce heat and add the ground peanuts gradually to the pan, mixing well.
- Simmer for 45 minutes until the meat is tender, stirring frequently to prevent the sauce from sticking to the bottom of the pan. Season.
- Add the green peppers, lime juice and dhania. If you desire a stronger peanut taste, add the peanut butter dissolved in a little hot water to form a paste. Heat through.
- Serve with rice, matoke (cooked banans) or creamed potatoes.

Serves 4

. . . .

Osso bucco

A relatively cheap but utterlly delicious recipe.

Ingredients

- 5 veal shanks or knuckles, cut into portions
- 3 carrots, diced
- 3 onions, finely sliced
- 8 tomatoes, peeled and liquidized
- 2 sticks celery, chopped
- 4 cloves garlic, crushed
- ½ cup oil

- 2 stock cubes dissolved in 2 cups hot water
- 1 cup dry red wine
- 4 tbsp plain flour
- ½ tsp fresh thyme (optional)
- salt and freshly milled pepper to taste
- parsley, chopped

Method

- Pre-heat oven to a moderate temperature.
- Sauté the onions, carrots and celery in 2 tbsp butter for about 5 minutes.
- Transfer to a casserole.
- Coat the veal lightly with flour and fry in the same pan with the remaining butter and oil on a medium flame until well browned.
- Put the shanks in the casserole containing the vegetables. Using the same fat, sauté the tomatoes in another pan for about 5 minutes.
- Add the stock, herbs, salt, pepper and garlic. Mix well. Then pour in the wine, reserving a little, and heat through well.
- Pour the sauce over the vegetables and meat. Add the remaining wine and some of the chopped parsley. Cover the casserole and place in the pre-heated oven for 1½ hours.
- Check the liquid level after 45 minutes and stir. If the veal is not genuine, it may take a bit longer. When done, garnish using the rest of the parsley. Serve with rice or noodles and bread.

Serves 4 – 6

. . . .

Beef stroganoff

A family must ... and to give it a Kenyan touch, add some freash dhania (corriander) at the end of cooking.

Ingredients

- 450 gm fillet steak, cut into thin strips
- 150 gm (5 oz) mushrooms, washed and sliced
- 2 large onions, thinly sliced
- 2 cloves garlic, crushed
- 1½ tbsp butter
- 1 tbsp vegetable oil
- 300 ml (½ pint) sour cream
- ½ cup wine
- 1 stock cube
- a dash of Worcestershire sauce
- 1 tbsp whole grain mustard
- 1 tsp corn flour mixed with a little water to thicken if needed
- salt and freshly milled pepper to taste

Method

- Heat the oil with the butter and fry the onions until clear.
- Add the garlic and meat over a high flame and fry for 1 minute.
- Add the mushrooms, wine, stock cube, seasoning and Worcestershire sauce. Allow to simmer for 5 minutes.
- Add sour cream and if necessary add the corn flour to thicken further. Allow it to cook on low heat for about 5 minutes.
- Check the seasoning, especially mustard. Garnish with dhania or parsley according to your preference. Serve with creamed potatoes or rice.

Hint: If the steak is tough, you may increase the cooking time, adding a little liquid (either wine or water).

Serves 4

. . . .

Marinated steak

Most "carnivores" that I know hate the idea of ruining the taste of a good steak by injecting foreign flavours in it. I agree with the sentiment to some extent. But sometimes it is not possible to attain the required flavour without the help of a good marinade.

Ingredients

- 500 gm (1 lb) fillet steak, sliced and beaten
- oil for frying
  For the marinade:
- ½ l (17.5 fl oz) yoghurt
- 2 tbsp oil
- 4 cloves garlic, crushed
- 1 tbsp ginger, crushed
- 1 tbsp paprika
- salt

Method

- Mix all the ingredients for the marinade together and add the steak, covering each slice completely. Let it marinate for at least 12 hours in the refrigerator.
- Remove the steaks from the refrigerator and allow to return to room temperature before frying in the oil. Alternatively, grill the steaks over a charcoal fire basting with oil as it cooks.

Hint: The secret to perfectly grilled steak is to control the coals so that they only glow. If flames appear, as they often do, have some water at hand to sprinkle onto the coal to douse the flames. Serve with a salad of your choice, garlic bread and baked potatoes.

Serves 4

. . . .

Beef Goan style

Goan food is interesting, although normally very hot.

Ingredients

- 1 kg (2.2 lb) rump steak, cubed
- 4 onions, chopped
- 4 cloves garlic, crushed
- 4 tomatoes, skinned and chopped
- 1 tsp tomato puree
- 1 tbsp ginger, crushed
- 1 stock cube dissolved in 2 – 3 cups hot water
- 2 tsp desiccated coconut
- 3 tbsp dhana jira, chopped (see glossary)
- red chillies
- ½ cup oil
- salt and freshly milled pepper

Method

- Fry the onions in the oil until almost golden.
- Add the meat and brown lightly, and then put in the tomatoes, garlic, ginger, dhania jira, tomato purée and desiccated coconut.
- After 3 minutes, add the stock cube, water and seasoning.
- Let it simmer for 45 minutes or until the meat is tender.
- Serve with rice.

Serves 4

. . . .

Chilli con carne

Has all the things we love in it.

Ingredients

- 100 gm red kidney beans, soaked overnight
- 400 gm (1 lb) minced meat
- 3 cloves garlic, crushed
- 3 onions, chopped
- 4 tomatoes, skinned and chopped
- 4 tbsp butter
- ½ tbsp oregano
- 2 bay leaves
- ¼ tsp paprika
- 2 stock cubes dissolved in 2 cups hot water
- about ½ bottle red wine
- 2 tbsp Worcestershire sauce
- a dash of tabasco
- ½ tsp sugar
- salt and freshly milled pepper

Method

- Fry the onions until clear, add the tomatoes and garlic and continue frying until soft.
- Mix in the minced meat, stirring briskly to avoid lumps, and turn up heat.
- Fry until all the liquid has evaporated. Stir in the wine, stock, herbs, paprika, sugar, tabasco, Worcestershire sauce, seasoning and beans.
- Lower heat, cover and allow to simmer for about 2½ hours. Correct the seasoning. Add a little more wine before serving and heat through.
- Serve with jacket potatoes, warm bread and a tomato and lettuce salad with basil.

Hint: To avoid lumpy mince meat, use a potato masher to break it up.

· · · · · · · · · · · · · · · · · · · ·

Pepper steak

Green pepper steak is delicious, but finding the peppercorns is a bit difficult. I have experimented with the local fresh ones but whatever I do, they still taste like plastic paint! For this reason I always use black pepper.

Ingredients

- 4 fillet steaks, sliced
- 4 tbsp butter
- 4 tbsp black peppercorns, crushed
- 3 tbsp brandy
- parsley or watercress to garnish

Method

- Coat the fillet steaks with the peppercorns, pressing hard.
- Over a medium to high flame, fry the steaks with the butter, lower heat and continue until they are cooked to your liking.
- If you like rare steaks, remove them earlier.
- Place the steaks in a separate serving platter, keeping them warm.
- Add cream to the same pan and as it heats up, add the brandy and try to ignite it. Pour this sauce over the steaks.
- Garnish and serve.

Serves 4

· · · · · · · · · · · · · · · · · · · ·

Roast fillet steak

An ideal way to cater for a cold lunch or picnic.

Ingredients

- 1 whole fillet steak, trimmed
  For the marinade:
- juice of 1 lime
- 3 tbsp olive oil
- 3 cloves garlic, crushed
- 1 tbsp crushed black pepper
- 1 sprig rosemary
- 2 onions, finely sliced

Method

- Mix the ingredients for the marinade together in a large bowl and place the whole steak in it.
- Let the steak marinate for at least 12 hours in the refrigerator, turning it from time to time.
- When ready to cook, allow it to return to room temperature. Pre-heat the oven to 250° C (gas mark 7).
- Wrap the steak in foil, moistened with some marinade and lay it in a baking tray. Place it in the oven and roast.
- After 20 minutes, unwrap the steak and baste it with the marinade.
- Cover it with the foil again and reduce the oven temperature. The steak should be done within an hour, but this depends on how well done you like it.
- Remove the foil for the last 10 minutes of cooking. Slice the steak finely before serving.
- Serve with potato salad or ratatouille and French bread.

Serves 4 – 6

. . . .

Veal liver

Properly cooked, veal liver is out of this world. Its delicate taste ensures that not too much needs to be done to it.

Ingredients

- 8 medium to thin slices veal
- 1 cup flour, seasoned with salt and pepper
- 1 tbsp butter
- 2 onions, sliced in rounds
- 1 punnet mushrooms, washed and sliced
- ½ cup cream

Method

- Soak the mushrooms in water with a little vinegar for 5 minutes then rinse with cold water.
- Dust the liver with the flour.
- Melt butter over a high flame and fry the liver rapidly. Normally they should be brown on the outside and pale pink inside, but if you prefer them well done, fry for a little while longer.
- Remove from the pan and keep hot in the oven. Fry the onions in the same butter, until slightly browned. Add the mushrooms and fry for 4 minutes.
- Pour in the cream and season.
- To serve, pour the mushroom sauce over the liver. Serve with creamed potatoes and a crisp green salad.

Serves 8

Blanquette of veal

This is a simplified version of the original recipe, but that does not mean it tastes less delicious.

Ingredients

- 1 kg (2.2 lb) veal cubes
- 6 slices smoked beef (optional)
- 2 onions, thinly sliced
- 4 sticks celery, chopped
- 2 stock cubes dissolved in 200 ml (8 fl oz) hot water
- 200 ml (8 fl oz) dry white wine
- ½ cup (double) cream
- 1 tbsp corn flour
- 4 tbsp butter
- ¼ tsp mixed herbs
- salt and freshly milled pepper
- parsley to garnish

Method

- In a heavy pan over a medium flame, melt the butter and sauté the onions and celery for 3 minutes.
- Add the veal and seal (see glossary for definition) for about 5 minutes without browning it.
- Add the stock, smoked beef and mixed herbs. Simmer until the veal is cooked, adding more water if it becomes too dry. This should take about 15 minutes.
- Pour in the wine and cook to reduce a little.
- Meanwhile, mix the cream and corn flour, lower the heat and stir it in with the veal.

Do not allow it to boil. Season and garnish with parsley just before serving.

- Serve with rice.

. . . .

Goulash

A kind of soup that is more than just soup; it is a meal.

Ingredients

- 1 kg (2.2 lb) rump steak, cubed
- 1 kg (2.2 lb) potatoes, peeled and cubed
- 60 gm (2 oz) bacon, diced (optional)
- onions, finely chopped
- 4 – 5 cloves garlic, crushed
- green peppers, washed, seeded and blanched
- 5 tomatoes, peeled and sliced

- stock cube, dissolved in 2 cups hot water
- 4 tbsp butter
- ½ cup red wine
- 2½ tsp paprika
- 1½ tsp caraway seeds
- tabasco
- Worcestershire sauce
- salt and freshly milled pepper to taste

Method

- Melt the butter in a large saucepan and sauté the onions until almost light brown. Add the meat and bacon, if preferred, caraway seeds and paprika.
- Brown the meat a little and then add the stock and garlic. Cover and simmer for about 1½ hours.
- Check the liquid content, adding water if needed. Add the tomatoes and potatoes, and simmer for 15 minutes.
- Pour in the wine with the green peppers and simmer for another 10 minutes. Put in a dash of tabasco and Worcestershire sauce with the other seasoning. If the liquid is too much, reduce the sauce in another pan and serve.
- Serve with garlic bread.

Serves 5

. . . .

Beef curry

We know the thin one.

Ingredients

- 1 kg (2.2 lb) rump steak, cubed
- 12 medium turnips, peeled and cubed
- 4 onions, sliced
- 4 cloves garlic, crushed
- 5 tomatoes, peeled and liquidized
- 1 tbsp ginger, crushed
- 1 beef stock cube dissolved in ¾ cup hot water

- ½ cup cream mixed with ½ tsp corn flour
- ½ cup oil
- 2 tbsp dhana jira
- ½ tbsp turmeric
- 1 tsp garam masala
- 1 bunch fresh dhania, chopped
- green chilies
- salt and freshly milled pepper
- extra dhania to garnish

Method

- Using a large, heavy-based pan, fry the onions in the oil until they turn light golden brown.
- Add meat and brown it.
- Add the tomatoes, dhana jira, turmeric, garlic and ginger.
- Continue to cook until most of the water has evaporated.
- Add stock, ½ the dhania, salt, pepper, chillies and turnips. Allow to simmer for about 1 hour or until the meat is tender.
- Check the liquid and add water if needed.
- Before serving, add the rest of the dhania and the gararn masala. Check the seasoning and stir in the cream.
- Heat through, but do not allow it to boil.
- Turn into a serving dish and garnish with dhania.
- Serve with rice.

Serves 6

Hint: If the meat is not tender, let it cook for a longer period before adding turnips.

. . . .

Boer kool

If you have never "gone Dutch", now is your chance to try your hand at it! I have "doctored" the original recipe for this dish as I am sure my Kenyan friends would find it too bland. This is Holland's version of our good old sukuma wiki.

Ingredients

- 1 kg (2.2 lb) potatoes, peeled and diced
- 20 bunches kale (*sukuma wiki* is fine), washed, destalked and chopped
- 1 l (36 fl oz) milk
- 1 packet beef or pork sausages, cooked and sliced
- 10 slices smoked beef bacon or ordinary bacon
- 4 tbsp butter
- ½ cup cream

- 1 stock cube, dissolved in ¼ cup hot water
- water for boiling
- salt and freshly milled pepper

Method

- Boil the potatoes and kale together until tender.
- Discard the water. Mash this mixture as finely as you can, adding milk, cream, seasoning; butter and stock.
- Return to the pan and heat slowly, stirring constantly to avoid it sticking to the bottom of the pan.
- Add the sausage and bacon. By now the mixture should be very thick and ready to serve. This meal is quite addictive in a strange, Dutch way. And since it is rather "heavy duty" stuff, serve it with a simple salad of lettuce and tomatoes.

Serves 4

. . . .

Chapter 5

Lamb

Highland Molo lamb chop stew

You may use beef if you wish, a real comfort food, that warms you through and again so easy quick and mzuri sana . . .

Ingredients

- ½ cup olive oil
- 2 onions sliced thinly
- 2 leeks chopped
- 4 cloves garlic
- 2 kg lamb chops
- 1 cup red wine
- 4 potatoes peeled
- 3 carrots halved
- 1 tbsp fresh thyme
- 1 litre chicken stock
- dash double cream (optional and add at the end of cooking)
- salt and pepper according to taste
- parsley to beautify

Method

- In a large pan, heat the oil and add the onions, leeks and garlic, sweat them for a few minutes, add the chops, turn the heat high, till they are browned a bit, add the wine, potatoes, carrots, thyme and stock.
- Let it boil for a minute, then cover and simmer, till tender, add salt and pepper and pili pili if you like, remove from heat and add the cream.
- Serve on warm platters, with ugali, rice or simply, as it is, wonderful . . .

Serves 4

. . . .

Nyama choma lamb chops

We have to marinate these for a while. You may use pork chops or even spare ribs if you wish. If you use spare ribs, boil these first for about thirty minutes to remove extra fat. Then continue, adding brown sugar and ketchup if you wish . . .

Ingredients

- 1 kg lamb chops beaten slightly
- 3 tsp crushed ginger
- 6 cloves garlic crushed
- 1 tsp curry paste or powder
- 1 tsp crushed cumin
- 1 tsp red chillies
- juice of 1 lime
- 4 tbsp yoghurt
- 2 tbsp olive oil
- (for the pork chops add 2 tbsp brown sugar and 2 tbsp ketchup)

Method

- Let these marinate for at least 6 hours, in the refrigerator.
- Remove an hour earlier before grilling.
- Baste with a little oil whilst you grill.
- Serve with potato salad, tamarind chutney, *kachumbari*. Another simple dip is to mix salt and red chilli with lime juice, or salt, chilli, chopped dhani and yoghurt, so simple so nice.

Serves 4

. . . .

Lamb stew

Ingredients

- 8 lamb chops
- 1 punnet mushrooms, washed and sliced potatoes, halved
- carrots, halved
- 8 onions, chopped
- 4 tbsp butter
- 1 cup cider
- 1 stock cube dissolved in 1½ cups hot water
- ¾ cup fresh cream mixed with ½ tsp corn flour
- ¼ tsp thyme
- ¼ tsp paprika
- ¼ cup parsley, chopped
- salt and freshly milled pepper
- parsley to garnish

Method

- Soak the mushrooms in water containing a dash of vinegar for 5 minutes and then rinse with cold water.
- Put the butter in a large pan and fry the lamb chops over a medium flame. Remove the chops from the pan.
- Lightly sauté the potatoes, mushrooms, onions and carrots together. Lower the heat and return the lamb chops to the pan.
- Add the stock, herbs, spices, seasoning and ¾ of the cider.
- Allow the stew to simmer for about 45 minutes, making sure the liquid does not dry completely.
- Add the parsley, cream and the rest of the cider. Simmer for a further 10 minutes
- Correct the seasoning. Skim off any excess fat and turn into a serving dish.
- Serve with butter-enriched ugali.

Hint: It is important to buy tender lamb chops for this recipe. If the lamb is tough, marinate it overnight in a little red wine with onions and the juice of 1 lime.

Serves 4

. . . .

Moussaka

A firm favourite on cold days.

Ingredients

- 1 kg (2.2 lb) minced lamb
- 500 gm (1 lb) aubergines thinly sliced. Sprinkle with salt, leave for 20 minutes and rinse.
- 3 onions, thinly sliced
- 3 cloves garlic, puréed
- 4 tomatoes, skinned and cubed
- 4 tbsp tomato purée
- 3 tbsp butter
- ¾ cup oil (mix equal portions of olive and corn oil)
- 3 tbsp corn flour
- 2 egg yolks
- ¼ tsp grated nutmeg
- ¼ tsp thyme
- salt and freshly milled pepper
- 200 ml (7 fl oz) white sauce (see glossary), cooled
- 25 gm (10 oz) cheese, grated

Method

- Lightly flour the aubergines.
- Melt the butter in a large, heavy-based pan. Fry the onions until they are clear.

- Add the garlic and the meat and continue to fry until the meat is well browned and no liquid is left.
- Put in the tomatoes with the nutmeg, thyme and other seasoning.
- Allow it to cook for about 15 minutes. Add the tomato purée and let it simmer for a few more minutes before removing the pan from the fire.
- In another pan, fry the aubergines in the oil in small batches, flouring them lightly with the corn flour until they turn slightly brown.
- Pre-heat the oven.
- Place ½ of the aubergines in a baking dish and spoon the meat mixture on top.
- Cover the meat with the remaining aubergines.
- Mix the white sauce with the egg yolk and pour over the aubergines, covering them completely.
- Sprinkle with the grated cheese and a little pepper and bake in a moderate oven for 40 minutes.

Serves 4

....

Ginger lamb chops

Be generous with the tangawizi.

Ingredients

- 8 medium lamb chops
- 2 onions, chopped
- 1 stock cube, dissolved in 4 cups hot water
- breadcrumbs
- 2 eggs, beaten
- oil for frying
  For the marinade:
- juice of 2 limes
- 1 tbsp ginger, crushed 1 tbs and cloves garlic, crushed
- salt and freshly milled pepper

Method

- Simmer the lamb chops with the onions and stock over a medium flame for 20 minutes. Remove from the fire and allow to cool.
- Mix the marinade ingredients in a large bowl and place the lamb chops in it, making sure they are well covered. Refrigerate for 12 hours, turning from time to time to ensure that the marinade completely covers the chops.
- When ready to cook, remove from the refrigerator and allow to return to room temperature. Coat the chops with the breadcrumbs, followed by the egg.
- Leave for 5 minutes on a tray. Repeat the coating process. Fry the chops over a medium flame in a frying pan until golden brown on both sides. If the chopshave "curled" and are difficult to shallow fry, you will have to deep-fry them.

Serve with ratatouille.

Serves 4

Lamb casserole

A hearty, wholesome meal.

Ingredients

- 450 gm (1 lb) lamb, cubed
- 2 cups haricot beans, soaked in water overnight
- 4 carrots, peeled and sliced
- 4 onions, chopped
- 4 tomatoes, skinned and sliced
- 3 sticks celery, chopped
- 2 leeks, sliced
- 2 tbsp butter
- 1 tbsp oil
- 1 stock cube dissolved in one cup of hot water
- ¼ tsp oregano
- ½ tsp paprika
- 2 bay leaves
- 1 tbsp tomato purée
- salt and freshly milled pepper

Method

- Boil the beans in salted water. After 20 minutes, drain and return to the fire with fresh boiling salted water for 2 more hours or until tender.
- In another pan, melt the butter and oil in a large, heavy-based pan and fry the onions and meat together.
- When lightly browned, add tomatoes and sauté further, followed by all the other vegetables. Add seasoning, herbs and stock.
- Allow to simmer for about 1 hour or until the meat is tender. Put in the beans and then the wine, reserving a little.
- When the meat is tender, season and pour in the reserved wine.

Serves 6

. . . .

Lamb in beer

Ingredients

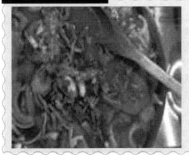

- 1 kg (2.2 lb) lamb, cubed
- 3 onions, chopped
- 1 clove garlic, crushed
- 2 tsp tomato purée
- 3 tsp butter
- 1 stock cube dissolved in 1 cup hot water
- 1 tsp corn flour
- 2 bay leaves

- ¼ tsp thyme
- 500 ml (16 fl oz) beer (reserve ¼ cup)
- 1 tsp soya sauce
- sugar (optional)
- salt and freshly milled pepper
- parsley

Method

- Fry the onions in the butter until clear, add the meat and brown.
- Mix the stock with the corn flour and add to the meat with the tomato puree, bay leaf, soya sauce, thyme, garlic and the beer, reserving ¼ of a cup.
- Simmer for about 40 minutes or until the meat is tender. Check the seasoning. If the taste is too sharp add a little sugar.
- Add the remaining beer. Serve with creamed potatoes.

Serves 4 – 5

. . . .

Roast leg of lamb

Ingredients

- 1½ kg (3 lb) leg of lamb
  For the marinade:
- 1 tbsp lime juice
- ½ cup red wine
- 2 tbsp olive oil
- ¼ cup yoghurt
- tbsp mixed herbs
- a small sprig of rosemary
- 8 cloves garlic, crushed

Method

- Mix the marinade ingredients well.
- Pour over the lamb and let it marinate in the refrigerator for at least 12 hours, turning it a few times.
- When ready to cook, allow it to return to room temperature.
- Pre-heat the oven to high (300°C).
- Place the lamb in a baking tin and put in oven with a little marinade, extra oil and about 1 cup of water. Reduce the temperature to 200°C after 20 minutes.
- Baste continuously with the marinade and add water, when necessary, a little at a time. The lamb should be cooked within 1¾ hours, depending on how well done you like it. Serve with sauté potatoes and mint sauce.

Serves 6

Lamb chops with rosemary

Ingredients

- 8 lamb chops, beaten lightly with a mallet
- 3 cloves garlic, crushed
- 1 tbsp fresh rosemary
- 4 tbsp lime juice
- 2 tbsp corn oil
- 5 tbsp olive oil
- 2 tbsp soya sauce
- ½ tsp cayenne pepper
- salt and freshly milled pepper

Method

- In a large dish, mix the lime juice, garlic, pepper, rosemary, and oil and soya sauce. Place the lamb chops in this marinade and leave for 6 – 8 hours in the refrigerator, turning occasionally.
- Grill the lamb chops under a medium flame for about 10 minutes each side, generously coating with the marinade to avoid it drying out.
- Sprinkle with salt to taste.
- Serve with jacket potatoes filled with melted cheese or beans in tomato sauce and yoghurt chutney.

Serves 4

Chapter 6

Seafood

Tandoori prawns (shrimp)

A simplified version of the original recipe but equally as good. The spices do not overpower the subtle taste of these magical prawns.

Ingredients

- 1 kg medium sized prawns, shelled and the black vein removed
- 2 tbsp butter with 1 tbsp corn oil
- 7 cloves garlic crushed
- 1 tbsp ginger crushed
- juice of two lemons
- 1 tsp ground coriander
- 2 tbsp ground cumin
- ½ tsp cayenne pepper
- ½ tsp paprika
- 1 tsp salt
- ¼ tsp each of ground cinnamon and cardamom

Method

- In a pan heat up the butter and oil. Add all the ingredients *except* the prawns. Let this froth up and sauté for a minute.
- Remove from heat and cool.
- Add the prawns and let them marinate for 2 hours. Place under a medium grill for about 2 minutes basting as you go.
- Serve with the marinade at the side with cocktail sticks. Now you know how restaurants make this dish. The difference being they may use charcoal to cook it.
- A perfect starter to any meal, finger food at its best.

Serves 4

. . . .

Scampi . . .

A revival of the 1960's. A lot of the food of the sixties and early seventies is coming back. That era was one not to be forgotten.

Ingredients

- 1 kg large shrimp, peeled and deveined
- 7 tbsp soft unsalted butter
- ¾ cup olive oil
- 2 tbsp Worcestershire sauce
- a dash of tabasco
- 12 cloves garlic minced
- 4 tbsp sweet sherry
- ½ tsp salt
- ½ tsp freshly milled pepper
- chopped parsley to add after cooking

Method

- In large bowl, add all the ingredients and mix well. Let this marinate for an hour in a cool place.
- Pre-heat the oven to 200°C. Place the shrimp with the marinade onto a tray and place in the oven.
- After about 8 minutes toss the shrimp around coating well and continue to cook for about 7 more minutes.
- The shrimp should turn pink, check to see if cooked through. If a little under done, put back into the oven for a few minutes.
- Sprinkle with parsley and serve as an appetiser, or with rich mash as a main course.

Serves 4

· · · · · · · · · · · · · · · · · · · ·

Malindi coconut fish

Simple to make, very coastal, use any firm fish like rock cod, kole or snapper.

Ingredients

- 1 kg of fish, marinated in the juice of two limes and 1 tsp of salt. Let rest for 20 minutes, rinse with water and pat dry
- 1 tbsp oil
- 3 chopped onions
- 1 tbsp cumin seeds
- 4 crushed cloves of garlic, the same amount of fresh ginger too
- 3 green chillies de-seeded
- 2 cups of coconut milk (use cans)
- salt and pepper to taste
- juice of 1 lime
- 1 cup chopped fresh coriander

Method

- Lightly fry the onions until golden, add the cumin seeds and fry for a minute, add garlic, ginger and green chillies.
- Add the coconut milk, season well adding the lemon juice, now do not try any further, top with lots of freshly chopped coriander.
- Serve with boiled rice … sometimes I just have it as a soup.

Serves 4

. . . .

Mombasa prawns in a gorgeous sauce

A sweet recipe that takes minutes. Devein the prawns and put in a salt mixture (1 tsp salt) for 20 minutes – this removes any fishy smell. Rinse well and pat dry.

Ingredients

- 2 onions finely chopped
- 1 cup finely chopped coriander
- 1 tsp cumin seeds
- 4 cloves garlic
- I tbsp ginger
- I tsp ground coriander
- ½ cup fresh mint leaves, chopped
- 1 de seeded green pepper chopped
- 3 green chillies
- ½ cup fresh coconut chopped
- 4 tbsp oil
- 800 gm peeled prawns, deveined and salted for 20 minutes and then rinsed well
- salt and pepper to taste

Method

- Blend the onions, coriander, cumin seeds, garlic, ginger, ground coriander, mint leaves, green pepper, chillies and coconut.
- Sauté this with the oil on a medium flame, mixing well and when this mixture begins to thicken, add the prawns.
- Now you really need to cook for about 4 to 5 minutes … no more!
- Serve with rice, nan bread, or even couscous. A cucumber salad dressed only with a little lemon juice, salt and pepper peps it up further. A great meal, fun to make and better still to eat.

Serves 4

Prawns Lamu style

Another wonderful recipe from the coast, full of flavours that only East Africa can be proud of ...

Ingredients

- 400 gm butter
- 3 red chillies
- 7 cloves garlic
- 1 tbsp ginger
- 1 tbsp whole cumin
- 1 tsp tomato ketchup
- dash lime juice
- salt and pepper to taste

Method

- Blend well, and this is your prawn butter ... Now for the rest ... 2 kg of prawns deveined and soaked in 1 tbsp of salt for 20 minutes and then rinsed.
- Melt the butter over a low heat in a pan, put your grill on full and lay the prawns on the tray, coat lovingly.
- As the prawns turn pink they are usually done ... check. Try not to overcook. Serve as a starter surrounded with crisp lettuce, or coleslaw. Simply heaven.

Serves 4 – 6

. . . .

Mombasa fish fritters

A delightful wonderful snack food eaten at the coast with coconut chutney, rare to find it elsewhere ...

Ingredients

- 500 gm rock cod or any firm fish fillet (snapper, perch or monkfish)
- ½ a tsp of (each) salt, pepper, cumin seeds, carom seeds (if available . . . generally Indian stores have them by the name of *ajaiwan*)
- 5 cloves of garlic crushed
- 2 tsp ginger crushed
- juice of 2 limes
- ½ cup of gram flour
- 1 tbsp self raising flour
- ½ tbsp plain flour
- little yoghurt
- oil for deep frying

Method

- Marinate the fish in the spices, combined with the garlic and ginger, for at least 20 minutes.
- Mix the 3 flours together with a little yoghurt (about ½ a cup) and add water to make a batter, rather a little thick than too watery.
- Dust the fish with some plain flour, that has been seasoned, dip the fish in the batter and deep fry till golden brown. Remember not to overcook. Fish can take up toonly 3 – 4 minutes to cook.
- Serve piping hot with coconut chutney, and look out at the sea.

· ·

Malindi coconut chutney

A very tiresome task that may be someone else can do for you…

Ingredients

- 2 freshly grated coconuts (brake the coconut, put it in the oven at 200°C for 20 minutes, with a knife, wedge the flesh against the shell and prize open, remove the dark brown skin and grate, or blend … adding:
- 2 bunches of coriander
- 2 – 4 green chillies … according to taste
- juice of 3 limes
- salt and pepper to taste

Method

- You must re-season this as it depends on the quantity of coconut to the lemons.
- A task it may be but watch the faces as they consume your product.

Serves 4

· ·

Prawns in love

A must for people who visit our country, for it is only here you will get such a dish that people keep asking for more and more.

Ingredients

- 3 tbsp oil
- 8 onions finely chopped
- 1 tbsp fresh ginger
- 1 tbsp fresh garlic
- 1 tbsp cumin

- 1 can tomatoes
- ½ tsp turmeric
- I kg prawns, cleaned and deveined
- some green chillies
- 250 ml water
- 1 tsp black pepper
- 1 tsp garam masala and 2 bunches coriander
     chopped
   salt and pepper

Method

- Sautee the onions utill golden brown, add the ginger, garlic, cumin, after a minute or so add the tomatoes, turmeric.
- Carry on cooking this till the sauce thickens . . . add water if too thick.
- Add the prawns, chillies, water (if needed) black pepper, garam masala, coriander, season with salt and pepper. Do not overcook ... generally once the prawns are pink, they are done. If unsure, simply re move one and cut in half and check. Better underdone at first rather than overcooked.
- Serve with rice, and or nan bread, enjoy as I love to say!

Serves 4

. . . .

Prawns in cider

Use dry cider for this boozy recipe. Do not overcook the prawns.

Ingredients

- 750 gm (24 oz) shelled prawns, cleaned and deveined
- 1 whole carrot, peeled and chopped
- 1 leek, chopped
- 600 ml (1 pint) cider
- 1 stock cube dissolved in 400 ml hot water
- ½ cup cream mixed with ¾ tbsp corn flour
- 1 tbsp butter
- 1 bay leaf
- salt and freshly milled pepper
- parsley to garnish

Method

- Pour the stock into a pan with the cider, reserving a little, and place over a medium fire.
- Add the butter, leeks, carrots and the bay leaf. Let this simmer for 15 minutes.
- Using a slotted spoon, remove the herbs and vegetables.

- Place the prawns in the pan and continue to simmer for 5 minutes.
- Add the cream and the reserved cider, season and heat through, but do not let it boil. When ready, garnish with parsley.
- Serve with rice or creamed potatoes and warm bread.

Serves 4

. . . .

Prawns in coconut . . . a fantastic Kenyan invention

Most people find making coconut milk difficult. Commercial coconut milk is available and if you find making your own inconvenient, you can go for it, although the taste is not as pleasant. Fish or chicken may also be used in this recipe.

Ingredients

- 1 kg (2.2 lb) fresh medium-sized prawns, cleaned and deveined
- 3 coconuts
- 4 onions, thinly sliced
- 4 tomatoes, skinned and sliced
- 2 green peppers, seeded, sliced and blanched
- 6 cloves garlic
- 2 tsp ginger, crushed
- 1 large bunch fresh dhania, chopped
- 2 stock cubes
- juice of one lime
- ½ cup oil
- 2 tsp cumin powder
- 1 l (35 fl oz) water

Method

To make coconut milk:

- Break the coconuts in half with a hammer (watch your hands!) and discard the liquid.
- Set your oven to a medium temperature and place the coconut, with the shell, onto the baking tray. Leave for 20 minutes.
- Separate the flesh from the shell with a blunt knife. It should come apart fairly easily. If it does not, return the coconut to the oven for another 10 minutes and try again.
- Grate the flesh finely.
- Place in a bowl and cover with hot (but not boiling) water. Let it stand for 10 minutes and sieve. The resulting thick fluid is the so called first extract of coconut "milk" and is the best. Some people extract more milk by adding hot water to the sieved flesh and repeating the process, but the resulting milk is thin and watery and, in my opinion, of little use.
- Alternatively, once you remove the flesh from the shell, you can liquidize it with warm water, a little at a time. Then sieve as before to extract the milk. Keep ¾ cup of the liquidised or grated flesh.

- Fry the onions in oil until they are nearly golden brown.
- Add the cumin, cook for 2 minutes then add the tomatoes, garlic and ginger. Lower heat and continue to fry until only the oil is left.
- Pour in the coconut milk and reduce. Add the stock cubes, prawns and lime juice. Simmer for about 20 minutes. Just before serving, add the green pepper and season. Garnish with lots of fresh dhania. Serve with rice.

Hint: To substitute the prawns with fish, first lightly poach it then cook just like the prawns. If substituting with chicken, first brown it lightly and then cook just like the prawns. It will, however, need to simmer for at least 50 minutes.

Serves 4 – 6

. . . .

Prawns paprika

Sometimes the paprika available is very hot. It should not be, so buy a well known brand.

Ingredients

- 2 kg (4.2 lb) medium-sized prawns, cleaned and deveined
- 3 onions, finely chopped
- 4 cloves garlic, crushed
- 2 tomatoes, skinned and chopped
- 1 tbsp tomato purée
- 1 stock cube dissolved in 2 cups hot water
- 1 cup cream mixed with 1 tbsp corn flour
- 2½ tbsp paprika
- a pinch of cayenne pepper or according to your taste
- 2 tbsp butter
- salt and freshly milled pepper
- ¼ bunch spring onions, chopped to garnish

Method

- Melt the butter and fry the onions over a medium flame until golden brown. Add the tomatoes, tomato purée and garlic and allow to cook for 5 minutes.
- Pour in the stock. Let this simmer for another 5 minutes.
- Add the prawns with cream, paprika, salt and pepper and stir. Cover and simmer gently for 15 minutes.
- Check the seasoning. Add cayenne pepper if liked. Turn into a serving dish and top with spring onions. Serve with rice or noodles accompanied by a plain green salad.

Serves 4

Prawns with lime and ginger

When you have several other dishes for the main course, this one is a quick and easy complement.

Ingredients

- 20 large prawns, cleaned and deveined
- 6 tbsp butter
- 1 bunch spring onions
- 2 cloves garlic, crushed
- 2 tbsp ginger, crushed
- juice of 3 limes
- ¼ cup water
- ¼ tsp cayenne pepper
- salt and freshly milled pepper

Method

- Melt the butter in a heavy pan over a medium flame.
- Add the prawns, lime juice and garlic and sauté for 2 minutes. Add the ginger and water, simmer for 5 minutes and season with salt, pepper, cayenne pepper and a little more lime juice.
- Check that the prawns are cooked, then turn the flame to high for one minute and add the spring onions.
- Serve with noodles.

Serves 4

....

Fish cooked in beer

This is quite a unique way of preparing fish. I once tried this recipe out on the shores of Lake Turkana.

Ingredients

- 6 fillets fish (sole or red snapper)
- 5 onions, finely sliced
- 3 cloves garlic, pureed
- 8 tomatoes, skinned and sliced
- 1 tsp tomato puree
- juice of 2 limes with a little of the rind
- 500 ml (6 fl oz) beer
- 4 tsp butter
- ¼ cup oil
- 1 stock cube
- salt and freshly milled pepper

Method

- Fry the onions until they are clear. Add the tomatoes and continue frying until the mixture looks like a puree, but do not burn.
- Add the garlic, lime juice rind and the beer, reserving ¼ cup.
- Boil until it reduces a little. Put in the stock cube, fish and tomato puree. Season and simmer for about 20 minutes.
- Correct the seasoning and pour in the remaining beer. Serve with rice or creamed potatoes.

Hint: You can also use tilapia or black bass, but whatever you use must be absolutely fresh, i.e. not frozen. To get rid of the "fishy" smell, soak the fish in milk for about 2 hours and then discard the milk.

Serves 6

· · · · · · · · · · · · · · · · · · · ·

Watamu fish thermidor

Ingredients

- 5 fish fillets
- 2 carrots, diced
- 1 cup mushrooms, washed and sliced
- 5 tbsp butter
- 1 clove garlic, crushed
- 2 tbsp corn flour
- 2½ cups milk
- juice of one lemon
- 1½ cups white wine
- ½ cup cream
- 1 stock cube (fish or chicken)
- ¾ cup cheddar che ese, grated
- 2 tbsp brandy
- ½ parmesan cheese
- ½ salt and freshly milled pepper
- breadcrumbs

Method

- Place the carrots in a large pan with about three cups of water or what you estimate will be just enough to cover the fish fillets (do not put the fillets in the pan just yet).
- Add the stock cube, lemon juice and wine.
- Bring to the boil and then reduce the heat, allowing the liquid to simmer. At this point add the fish fillets and poach for 5 minutes.
- Remove using a slotted spoon and keep warm on a platter.
- Over a medium heat, melt the butter; add the garlic and mushrooms and sauté for a few minutes.

- Add the flour and cook, stirring constantly, for one minute. Remove from heat and gradually add milk and cream, stirring well.
- Return the pan to the fire. The mixture should thicken.
- Season, then reduce the heat and add the cheddar cheese, stirring continuously.
- Pour in the brandy and heat through without boiling.
- Place the fish in a buttered casserole and pour the sauce over it.
- Sprinkle with breadcrumbs and a little parmesan cheese.
- Bake in a moderate oven for 20 minutes.
- Brown under the grill if necessary.

Hint: Lobster may be used in this recipe instead of fish. Alternatively, you can make it a seafood mix.

Serves 5

. . . .

Lobster with cream

If possible, buy live lobsters. (See glossary on how to prepare lobster for cooking).

Ingredients

- 1 kg (2.2 lb) lobster
- 1 cup mushrooms, washed and sliced
- 3 tbsp butter
- ¾ cup dry white wine
- 300 ml (10 fl oz) cream
- ½ tbsp corn flour
- juice of 1 lime
- a pinch salt and freshly milled pepper
- a pinch cayenne pepper
- parsley to garnish

Method

- Remove the lobster meat from the claws and tail by holding the head and tail firmly in each hand. Twist, use napkins to hold the lobster if the body is prickly. The tail should come off, pulling the meat with it. Use a small knife to separate the meat from the cavity. If you cannot manage, ask your butcher to show you how to do it.
- Cut the lobster flesh into 2 – 3 cm slices.
- Melt the butter over a high flame and fry the mushrooms with the lobster, stirring rapidly.
- Add the wine and allow to bubble for 2 minutes. Meanwhile, mix the cream with the corn flour. Lower heat and add the cream mixture.
- Let it simmer for 15 minutes.
- Add lime juice. Season and garnish. Serve with plain rice or new potatoes.

Hint: Remove the lobster flesh, concentrating on the claws and tail. A kitchen hammer is helpful. When doing this for the first time, it may seem difficult but with time and practice, it becomes manageable.

Serves 2 – 3

· · · · · · · · · · · · · · · · · · · ·

Lobster mayonnaise

Ingredients

- 1 kg (2.2 lb) lobster, boiled and flesh removed and cubed
- 1 cos lettuce, washed
- 200 gm (8 oz) mayonnaise
- 1 tbsp tomato purée
- 1 onion or ½ bunch spring onion, finely chopped
- 1 clove garlic, crushed
- 1 tbsp lime juice
- 1 tbsp brandy
- juice of 1 lime
- 1 tsp whole grain mustard
- paprika
- salt and freshly milled pepper
- parsley to garnish

Method

- Mix the mayonnaise with all the ingredients except the lobster, seasoning and the lettuce. Then gently mix in the lobster and season according to your taste.
- Arrange the lettuce on a platter and spoon the lobster mixture onto it.
- Chill and garnish just before serving.
- Serve with a mixed salad and slices of avocado.

Hint: Since no cooking is required for this recipe, boil the lobster for at least 10 minutes.

Serves 3

· · · · · · · · · · · · · · · · · · · ·

Fish mauniére

Ingredients

- 4 fish fillets (sole or red snapper), of medium thickness
- 185 gm (6 oz) butter
- plain flour
- ½ cup lime juice
- parsley
- salt and freshly milled pepper

Method

- Lightly dust the fish fillets with flour.
- Melt ½ the butter in a heavy pan over a medium flame.
- Fry the fillets for about 3 minutes on each side and place them aside on a platter and keep warm.
- Melt the rest of the butter and add the lime juice, pepper and parsley.
- Pour this sauce over the fish. Serve immediately.

Hint: You can use any kind of fish as long as it is not oily. Serve with creamed potatoes and sautéed tomatoes.

Serves 4

. . . .

Trout meuniére

Ingredients

- 4 trout, whole
- 1 cup plain flour seasoned with salt, pepper and parsley
- ¼ cup almonds, blanched and skinned
- juice of 2 limes
- parsley
- ½ a bunch of spring onions chopped
- 4 tbsp butter mixed with 1 tbsp oil
- freshly milled pepper

Method

- Clean trout, removing the insides and the head.
- Dust lightly with the flour and fry in butter over a medium heat for about 5 minutes each side.
- Set the fish aside on a warm platter.
- Add the lime juice, parsley, spring onions, pepper and almonds to the butter in the pan.
- Heat gently and pour over the fish.
- Serve with creamed potatoes, sautéed snow-peas or mushrooms and a green salad.

Hint: As trout has its own distinctive taste, the vegetables served with it should only be mildly seasoned, if at all.

Serves 4

. . . .

Deep-fried calamari

Cleaning calamari may seem difficult. Ask your butcher to show you how to do it, and you will soon master it.

Ingredients

- 1 kg (2.2 lb) calamari, sliced into medium-sized rings
- 2 eggs, beaten with a little milk and seasoned with salt and pepper
- breadcrumbs
- oil for deep frying

Method

- Coat the calamari with the egg and then roll it in the breadcrumbs.
- Heat the oil and deep-fry the calamari in batches for about 2 minutes or until done.
- Serve with lime wedges, garlic mayonnaise, and home-made tomato sauce or herb mayonnaise (see subsequent recipes).

Hint: It is quite easy to clean calamari. Gently pull the head off and most of the insides should come out too. If some of the insides remain, use plenty of running water and a pointed knife to remove them, ensuring that the ink sac and transparent bone are not left inside. Peel off the outer skin, washing it well to get rid of hidden grit. You may use the tentacles if you wish, but they are often tough and not worth using.

Serves 4

Chapter 7

Vegetables and Assorted Accessories

The variety of vegetables available is wide, and they can be delicious if prepared creatively. Vegetables like broccoli, snow-peas and French beans can be boiled briefly, with the addition of a little bicarbonate of soda at boiling point to preserve the colour. Then sauté with garlic, onions, salt and pepper. This may look simple, but the addition of too much cream, cheese or even garlic often renders a flavour that is overwhelming and the vegetables lose their character.

Sukuma sauce

A tasty blend of spinach and spices, all you have to do is sauté your favourite meat, paneer, or seafood to this mix. Cook 1 day ahead, refrigerate and use the next day. The flavour will develop to your delight! 10 big bunches sukuma, cleaned, dropped in boiling salted water for 10 minutes, then drained and rinsed quickly in cold water. You may puree the sukuma or just chop it finely ... as you prefer.

Ingredients

For the sauce:
- ¼ cup oil
- 4 medium onions finely chopped
- 2 tsp cumin seeds
- 1 tsp coriander powder
- 2 tbsp fenugreek leaves (optional ... available from Indian spice shops)
- 8 cloves garlic crushed
- 1 tbsp ginger grated finely
- 3 tomatoes chopped
- 1 tbsp tomato puree
- 3 green chillies chopped (more or less according to taste)
- 2 bunches fresh coriander washed and leaves finely chopped
- salt and pepper to taste
- ¼ cup double cream
- 3 cm piece of ginger

Method

- Over a medium heat, place the oil in a pan and sauté the onions till light brown, add the cumin, coriander powder, fenugreek leaves, garlic and ginger, stir-fry this till you smell the spices (about 2 minutes) then add the tomatoes and continue to fry till tender.
- Add the tomato paste, green chillies, coriander, salt and pepper.
- Add the spinach and the meat, paneer or seafood.
- Check the seasoning, add the double cream, and peel an extra 3 cm piece of fresh ginger and cut into very very fine strips and garnish just before serving. Ever so versatile and you can freeze it too.

Serves 4

. . . .

Some other marinades for meat or chicken

Remember to let your meat or chicken marinate in these for at least 24 hours, then simply grill the meat, basting as you go.

Fruity marinade

Ingredients

- ½ cup pineapple juice
- 5 tbsp basalmic vinegar
- 4 tsp brown sugar
- 2 tsp olive oil
- 1 clove garlic
- 1 tsp paprika
  Meaty marinade
- ½ a cup Worcestershire sauce
- 5 tbsp teriyaki sauce
- 4 tsp honey
- 2 tsp olive oil
- ¼ tsp each of thyme, oregano and sage
- 2 cloves garlic crushed
- 1 tsp sesame oil
  Yoghurt marinade
- ½ cup natural yoghurt
- 4 cloves garlic crushed
- 4 tsp ginger pounded
- 1 tbsp lemon juice
- 1 tsp ground cumin
- 4 tsp olive oil
- 1 tsp paprika

Hint: If you require more, double the quantity.

Serves 4

Peperonade

A tasty sauce for grilled fish. If the different coloured peppers are not available, use what is.

Ingredients

- 3 tbsp extra virgin olive oil
- 4 onions finely chopped
- a good pinch saffron
- a good pinch cayenne pepper
- 3 cloves garlic crushed
- 3 tomatoes crushed
- 1 tbsp tomato puree
- ½ a cup white wine
- 1 green pepper
- 1 red or yellow pepper
- salt and pepper to taste
- good pinch sugar

Method

- On a medium heat fry the onions till just a little golden, then add the saffron, cayenne pepper and garlic.
- Sautee this for a minute then add the rest of the ingredients. If the sauce is too thick add a little water.
- Make sure you let the wine evaporate, by heating the sauce for a few minutes. As a variation you may add basil. Vegetarians can coat asparagus, artichoke hearts, in fact whatever you please.

Serves 4

Thai marinade

An authentic marinade good with chicken, fish or shrimp. Remember that at least 1 hour is needed for marinating.

Ingredients

- 1 cup coconut milk
- 1½ bunch coriander
- 7 cloves garlic crushed
- 4 tbsp ginger chopped
- ¼ cup fish sauce
- juice of two limes
- 2 tbsp dark sugar
- 2 fresh chillies chopped
- 1 small onion chopped
- ¼ cup oil

Method

- Place the above ingredients in a food processor and blend till smooth.
- Smother the chicken, fish, etc. with the sauce and put in the refrigerator for an hour. Remove about 20 minutes before you intend to use it.
- Place under a grill, basting as you go.
- Remember that fish and shrimp need not much time for cooking. As a guide 4 minutes per side, but check with a knife as this really does depend the thickness.

Serves 4

. . . .

Sweet cornbread

We in Kenya eat polenta all the time. It is just another name for ugali! I do think polenta may be ground a little finer. Ugali is savoury, this 'bread' is sweet, a recipe from the USA.

Ingredients

- 250 gm yellow or white polenta (corn meal)
- 125 gm self raising flour
- 125 gm corn flour
- 180 gm sugar
- 1 tsp rounded baking powder
- 90 gm butter (keep 1 tsp apart for later use)
- 375 ml milk, warmed
- 2 eggs beaten
- ½ cup sultanas plumped up in a warm cup of tea, drained after ½ an hour and pat dry
- a pinch of salt
- a good pinch cinnamon

Method

- Put your oven on 180°C, place the cornmeal in a large bowl, with the self raising flour, corn flour, sugar, and baking powder.
- Melt the butter, add the milk, bring just to warm, remove from heat.
- Add the eggs and whisk, blend with the flour mixture, with the sultanas, salt and cinnamon.
- Place in a baking tray and bake till a golden brown, about 25 minutes or so. Remove, brush with remaining butter and serve.
- You may like it warm or cold, with butter, jam, clotted cream, even a little whipped cream with some good chunky jam on top.

Serves 4

. . . .

Rosti

A potato dish from Switzerland, quite addictive and great with many main

Ingredients

- ½ kg potatoes, boiled untill ½ cooked, peeled,
    then grated on the largest holes on a grater
- 2 onions very finely chopped
- salt and pepper to taste
- oil to just cover the bottom of a non stick pan

Method

- Mix the potatoes with the onions, season well and make into little 'burgers', flatten them a little.
- Place oil in a non-stick pan and on a medium to low flame or heat, place the 'burgers', into the pan.
- Turn the 'burgers' after about 12 minutes or so. You may lift them slightly to see if they have browned.
- When both sides are done, remove, place on kitchen paper and serve straight away. These go well with almost any meal you plan ... roast chicken, *nyama choma*, steaks, fish and even other vegetarian dishes for those who do not like meat. A must try recipe for Kenyan homes.

Serves 4

....

Tamarind chutney with dates

Great with all curries and cold meats, dip tacos or papadums in it too. Another Kenyan hero.

Ingredients

- 80 gm tamarind seeds removed
- 500 gm dates pips removed
- 500 ml boiling water
- juice of ½ a lime
- 2 tsp toasted cumin seeds (just dry roast on a pan, with medium heat till you smell the spice ... do not burn it.
- ½ bunch fresh coriander chopped
- salt, red chilli and sugar to taste

Method

- Place the tamarind and dates in a pan with the hot water and simmer. Try to 'break' up the mixture and soften it.
- Put this through a medium sieve (it seems hard but you may add a little water to help along).

- Add the lime juice, cumin, coriander and season according to your taste.
- Sometimes a little grated carrot can be added or diced onion too. Chill well and you can serve this alongside samosas, bhajias as well.

Serves 4

· · · · · · · · · · · · · · · · · · · ·

Mango salsa

Such lovely mangoes we have. This is an exotic way to make a chutney that goes well with cold meats, curry or in sandwiches to pepper them up.

Ingredients

- 4 medium, firm (just ripe) mangoes
- juice of 3 limes
- zest of 1 lime (organic) or omit
- 2 green chillies minced
- 2 red chillies minced
- 1 onion very finely diced
- 2 tsp freshly grated ginger
- 1 bunch fresh coriander chopped
- ½ bunch parsley chopped
- 250 ml good olive oil
- 2-3 tsp sugar
- 1 cardamom, pod removed and seeds sprinkled (optional)
- salt and freshly milled pepper

Method

- Mix all the ingredients together, check seasoning and chill. For an added crunch place ½ sliced cucumber in a bowl with salt and leave for 30 minutes.
- Rinse, dry and add to the salsa at the last minute.

Serves 4

· · · · · · · · · · · · · · · · · · · ·

BBQ sauce

Ideally for spare ribs, chicken wings, steaks, let the meat marinate overnight for better results.

Ingredients

- ½ cup oil
- 2 onions finely chopped
- 3 cloves garlic crushed
- 1 tbsp ginger
- I can crushed tomatoes

- 1 tsp corn flour, little water dissolved in a little water ... just before us
- I stock cube (beef or chicken) dissolved in a little water
- 3 tbsp red wine vinegar (or of your choice)
- 3 tbsp Worcestershire sauce (lea and perrins)
- 1 tbsp mango or tomato chutney (available ready made in stores)
- 2 tbsp honey (increase this or decrease it as you like)
- 2 tbsp lime juice
- 1 tsp thyme
- ½ tsp celery salt
- later salt and pepper to taste, with an option to add some cayenne if liked

Method

- On a medium flame heat the oil in a pan, add the onions and sauté till clear, add the garlic and ginger and fry for a minute.
- Add the tomatoes, take off the heat for a minute and add all the rest of the ingredients, stir well and resume heating and stir all the time, check the seasoning and the sweetness and sharpness, adjust as you would like it.
- Remove from the heat once the sauce is sticky and a little thick. Now cool and marinate your meat of choice for at least 6 hours or overnight, whichever is preferable.
- Makes up 4 portions.

. . . .

Sukuma wiki (spinach) with oyster sauce

Ingredients

- 500 gm spinach, cooked in salted boiled water, for 4 minutes. Drain.
  In another large pan, add:
- 2 tsp oil
- 3 tsp sesame oil
- 3 red or green chillies chopped
- 3 cloves garlic, chopped
- 2 tsp ginger
  Stir fry this for about 2 minutes, then add:
- 60 ml oyster sauce
- 60 ml dry sherry
- 60 ml light soy sauce
- 1 tbsp honey
- a handful of chopped nuts of your choice
- salt and pepper to taste

You can use leftover spinach and create another dish at hardly any cost...
- Add the spinach and heat.
- Serve with ugali, rice or mash.

Serves 4

. . . .

Glazed carrots

A must for some odd reason, I think it is the sweetness and the colour combination that makes this vegetable ever so befitting for this special occasion . . . Christmasy, if there were such a word.

Ingredients

- 1½ kg medium-sized carrots, peeled
- 50 gm butter
- 2½ tbsp sugar
- 1 onion cut into thin rounds
- 2 pinches bicarbonate of soda
- 1 bunch parsley chopped
- salt and freshly ground pepper

Method
- Place the carrots in a pan, on a medium heat and pour some boiling water (from the kettle) just covering them.
- Add the butter, sugar, onions and bicarbonate of soda.
- Cook till tender and the liquid has reduced and is syrup like. If the carrots are done faster, remove them and continue to reduce the liquid. Season well and add the chopped parsley.
- Serve on a warmed platter.

Serves 8

. . . .

Festive sweet potatoes

A magical touch for a magical time of year with a Kenyan flair.

Ingredients

- 1½ kilo sweet potatoes, peeled and cut into 1 cm rounds
- 50 gm butter (unsalted)
- 120 ml golden syrup
- 1 tsp freshly grated ginger
- 1 tbsp lime or lemon juice
- sprinkle of salt and freshly ground black pepper
- chopped parsley to sprinkle at the end

Method

- Boil the sweet potatoes for 10 minutes, drain.
- In a pan, melt the butter over medium heat and stir in the golden syrup, ginger and lemon juice.
- Pre-heat the oven to 190°C.
- Grease a large baking dish and place the sweet potatoes overlapping them.
- Drizzle over the syrup mixture and bake for 3 minutes or till tender. About half way, baste over with a spoon.
- Sprinkle over with the parsley. You may like to cook this half way and make way for the Turkey or Gammon and then replace it afterwards – ready in time for the rest of the meal.

Serves 8

. . . .

Jewelled couscous

Almonds, pistachios, plump sultanas and a final sprinkle of pomegranate make this dish a very special kind of stuffing, without hassle . . . and yes pour gravy over it, it is utterly delicious.

Ingredients

- 500 gm couscous, cooked according to instructions on pack. Instead of just water, add a couple of stock cubs dissolved in the water and a good pinch of saffron. Omit the salt
- 1 cup almonds and pistachio nuts, chopped
- 1 cup sultanas, soaked in warm water for an hour
- 1 bunch chopped parsley
- 1 bunch chopped mint
- 6 tbsp melted butter to incorporate at the end
- 1 shelled pomegranate to sprinkle right at the end (get the kids to do this)

Method

- Once the couscous is cooked (it only takes minutes) separate gently with a fork as you would with rice.
- Add all the other ingredients except the pomegranate, which you sprinkle on top and around.
- Another 'dish' that you can prepare in advance and not fret, giving you time for other chores in the kitchen.
- For that extra Christmas feel, drizzle a little honey over the couscous and scatter some golden brown onion rings around – now that is festive.

Serves 8

. . . .

Homemade muesli . . . another variation

It is fresher, wholesome, cheaper and better than those factory packs. This recipe is for two, so multiply by the portions required. Also add other fruit like grapes, oranges, mangoes, passion and pineapple. We have an abundance of fabulous fruit in Kenya.

Ingredients

- 1 cup rolled oats, toasted slightly under the grill and soaked in apple juice or orange juice for a few minutes ...
  Add:
- 2-3 tbsp honey
- juice of 1 lime
- ¼ cup fresh coconut flakes
- ½ cup strawberries or fruit of your choice
- ½ cup toasted almonds or cashews
- 1 peeled apple, cored and grated or sliced
- ½ cup sultanas plumped up in some warm water for 15 minutes (drained)
- good sprinkling of lightly roasted nuts (pistachios cashews, almonds, etc.)
- ice cold milk, to serve with (or good Greek organic yoghurt)

- If you are on a diet, omit the honey and add your sweetener.
- For even a fruitier kick, add some good quality strawberry or raspberry jam.

Serves 2

. . . .

Rosti potatoes

The ideal potato dish for breakfast, lunch and dinner. Add a little garlic to the oil, remove before it browns.

Ingredients

- 3 large potatoes, washed well and boiled, skin on for 12 minutes, cool, peel and grate using the largest hole in grater (they must be cold when you grate them)
- salt and pepper to taste
- ½ cup olive oil

Method

- Lightly season the potatoes. Do not mush them. Form into hamburger like shapes not too thick though.

- Heat a non-stick pan on medium heat and place the oil in it. When hot, add the shaped potatoes and let turn golden brown and crispy. Do not let the heat get too high.
- Flip over and repeat the process.
- As a variation you may add a grated onion too.
- At breakfast these will go well with your eggs, bacon, sausage, and tomato, or with cold cut meats at lunch and a roast for dinner.
- It is extremely versatile and what Icall food friendly … have it in slightly warmed bread, dripping in butter (or olive oil) a kind of sandwich … I warn you it is addictive, but ever so nice.

Serves 4

. . . .

Sweet potato gratin

We make gratin(s) out of ordinary potatoes. I had it once made with sweet potatoes and thought to try it out. This recipe that translates locally available product to international standards with pomp. You layer everything as you would with lasagne.

Ingredients

- 8 medium sweet potatoes, peeled and sliced as thin as possible
- 4 onions peeled and sliced into thin rounds
- 350 gm good cheddar cheese
- 600 ml double cream
- good pinch cayenne pepper
- salt and freshly ground pepper
- good knob of butter

Method

- Butter a casserole dish and layer the sweet potato, adding a little onion here and there, add cheese, salt and pepper. Repeat. The last or rather the top layer should
  have the cream and cayenne pepper mixed, and some cheese too.
- Bake covered in an oven at 180° C for 20 minutes, then uncover and bake for 15 minutes or till golden brown, bubbly and tender.
- Serve piping hot with nyama choma (BBQ) roasts, stews or juicy steaks. Truly a dish that will take your breath away – so to speak.

Serves 4 – 6

. . . .

Raspberry snow-peas

A unique flavour that I first tried when I was in the USA. I admit that I had to ask for the recipe, but now at least I share it.

Ingredients

- ½ kg snow-peas top and tailed
- 8 tbsp raspberry vinegar (if not available squash a good handful of fresh raspberries and place with 8 tbsp white wine vinegar)
- 6 tbsp toasted sesame seeds (dry roast in a pan until they turn a very light brown)
- a drizzle of honey
- salt and pepper to taste

Method

- In a pan, boil enough water for the snow-peas. Add ½ tsp of salt and place the snow peas in it.
- Cook to your liking, remove from heat, drain and immediately place in a dish with the vinegar.
- Season with salt and pepper, sprinkle the sesame seeds, and drizzle the honey over. Serve with your main course. A brilliant rainbow of flavours that blend very well.

Serves 4

. . . .

Grilled aubergine (eggplant)

Here in Kenya, have an abundance of aubergine at affordable prices. In this recipe we first bake the aubergine, followed by grilling and then marinating. Not complicated just a few easy steps to a grand appetizer.

Ingredients

3 medium sized aubergines, top and tail them, and slice into about 2 cm rounds. Pre-heat oven to 200° C. Place the aubergine on an oiled tray and bake for about 12 minutes. Remove and place under a medium grill till tender. Keep warm.

Marinade ...
Mix the following ...

- ½ cup virgin olive oil
- ½ cup white wine
- ½ cup red wine vinegar
- 4 cloves garlic crushed
- ¼ tsp oregano (dried)
- ¼ tsp thyme (dried)
- good pinch cayenne pepper
- salt and pepper to taste

Method

- Layer the aubergine in a casserole, and pour the marinade over.
- Leave in the refrigerator for as long as possible, preferably overnight. Check seasoning and correct if necessary.
- Serve as an appetizer or a side dish alongside your main course. A butterly, delicious dish that only dreams are made of!

Serves 4

. . . .

Tasty asparagus

We have absolutely wonderful asparagus here in Kenya. It is often smothered in butter or hollandaise. This time it is going to be plain, simple but very good.

Ingredients

- ½ kg asparagus trimmed (simply hold the asparagus with both hands midway and snap)
- ¼ cup sesame oil
- 5 tbsp sesame seeds, toasted in a dry pan till they turn very light brown
- salt and pepper to taste
- dash lemon
- drizzle of honey
- some chopped parsley

Method

- Place a pan of salted water on high heat and boil, cook until tender (this varies alot due to the thickness or thinness of the asparagus, so check after 5 minutes).
- Drain and rinse under cold water.
- Dry lightly on a kitchen towel.
- Place on a dish, drizzle the sesame oil, season with salt and pepper, drizzle again with the honey and sprinkle some chopped parsley on top. This brings out the essence of asparagus, I think. I hope you too are pleased with it.

Serves 4

. . . .

Stir fried corn, Nakuru style

My aunty in Nakuru, who has since died gifted me with this recipe. I have over time collected many recipes from ailing relatives to preserve their secrets and for us to enjoy and remember them fondly. There could be no better tribute to their memory, I think ...

Ingredients

- 6 medium sized soft corn cobs (remove the kernels by holding the corn upright and slicing them off with a sharp knife)
- ½ cup corn oil
- 2 cloves garlic crushed
- 1 tbsp ginger crushed
- ½ tsp cayenne pepper
- 2 tbsp lime juice
- 1 – 2 tsp sugar
- salt and pepper to taste

Method

- Place the oil in pan on medium heat. When almost smoking, cautiously add the corn, stir fry for about 5 minutes reduce heat add all the other ingredients and cook until done (about another 15 minutes). If the mix becomes too dry add a little water. Check seasoning.
- Place in a sieve to drain the oil, lightly shake the sieve to remove excess.
- Serve alongside your favourite stews, *nyama choma* or curry. An added favourite could be some cumin seeds thrown in with the garlic and ginger, topped off with some fresh coriander right at the end. It gives a nice crunch to your meal and is wonderfully glorious. Truly a Kenyan dish.

Serves 4

. . . .

Garlicky spinach

A perky stir fry, sure to please and so good for you. As an additional complement add a good spoonful of double cream to it at the end of cooking. Quick, simple and beautifully wicked.

Ingredients

- 1 kg spinach, washed, spun dry and patted with kitchen paper
- 2 tbsp sesame oil plus 1 tsp corn oil
- 10 cloves garlic crushed (less if you wish)
- 1 tsp soy sauce
- 2 tbsp sesame seeds, lightly dry toasted in a pan over a medium heat until light
- brown ... sprinkled on just before serving

Method

- In a large pan over high heat, add the oil and as soon as it smokes add the garlic and spinach.
- Stir fry rapidly till the leaves wilt, stir in about a tbsp of soy sauce, remove from heat, put on a platter and sprinkle the sesame seeds. Serve immediately.
- As an alternative, try a little ginger, 1 tsp of sugar and a good pinch of cayenne pepper to this dish. Need I tell you that you could use *sukuma wiki* though it may need extra stir frying time and that it is healthy? A firm favourite that never fails to satisfy, young and old alike.

Serves 4 – 6

. . . .

Special spinach bake

A wholesome, healthy and tasty family dish. It is comfort food at its best.

Ingredients

- 300 gm spinach blanched and squeezed dry (drop in boiling salted water and when the water returns to the boil remove and cool with additional cold water)
- 8 large potatoes boiled with skin on, then peeled and broken up roughly
- 1 cup double cream
- 6 spring onions chopped
- 2 cloves garlic crushed
- ¼ cup butter
- good sprinkle of nutmeg
- 1 tsp salt
- 1 tsp freshly milled pepper
- 1½ cup cheddar (to sprinkle on top later)

Method

- Pre-heat the oven to 200°C. Combine all the ingredients in a bowl except for the cheese. Check the seasoning and correct if needed.
- Place in a casserole dish and bake for 15 minutes.
- Remove, sprinkle the cheese on top and bake for another 5 minutes or until bubbling away. A superb heart warming happy dish.

Serves 4

. . . .

Oriental carrots, Kenya style

Good for your eyes and therefore good for you ... enriched, this simple recipe helps kids to enjoy vegetables.

Ingredients

- 500 gm salted, boiling water
- 1 tbsp sugar
- 2 cloves garlic crushed
- 1 tsp cumin dry, roasted in a pan until it smells good do not burn
- 1 tsp paprika
- 1 juice of one lemon
- 500 gm carrots, sliced

Method

- Add all these ingredients and boil for 10 minutes or until just tender, drain and add in a pan.
  - 2 tbsp olive oil
  - 1 tsp tomato puree
  - good sprinkle of garam masala
  - dash chilli sauce or even a fresh chilli cut up
  - pepper and salt to taste
  - some freshly chopped coriander
- Stir fry for a few minutes, checking the seasoning, for a little elaboration add a good ½ cup of double cram at the end – do not boil – bet the eyes will look great after this.

Serves 2

. . . .

Marinated grilled vegetables

For this recipe, use brocoli, cauliflower, mushrooms, carrots and squash. Remember that you need to leave an hour for marinating. If you need a bigger quantity, simply double all the marinade ingredients. Make the vegetables into bite size bits and grill for about 15 minutes. You can of course use your charcoal grill or the normal electric/gas grill. Marinade.

Ingredients

Marinade:
- 4 tbsp basalmic vinegar
- 4 tbsp red wine
- 1 cup good olive oil
- 7 cloves garlic crushed
- ½ a tsp mustard
- ½ a bunch fresh basil, chopped
- good grind of freshly milled black pepper.

Method

- Mix well and pour over your vegetables, let sit for an hour.
- Grill over medium to low heat. If there is too much marinade, reserve the extra and use up next time. It will keep for a week in the refrigerator.
- Add salt at the end of cooking. I find these incredibly tasty, sprinkle some parmesan cheese to take it further.

Serves 6

. . . .

Spinach with flavour

Sometimes wonderful food can be simple, but delectable, this recipe surely is.

Ingredients

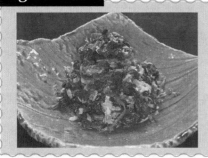

- 2 tbsp oil
- 3 onions finely diced
- 4 tsp ginger grated
- 4 cloves garlic crushed
- 130 ml coconut cream
- 1 green chilli minced
- a good pinch salt and pepper
- 5 bunches spinach, washed and diced

Method

- In a pan heat the oil, add the onions and brown, then throw in the ginger and garlic, add the coconut cream, and chilli. If the mixture is too thick add a little stock.
- Mix in the spinach. Let cook till tender. Serve hot alongside your main course, quite heart warming.

Serves 2

. . . .

Cabbage and *sukuma wiki* "pie"

Sukuma is the local spinach,(if not available use any good spinach)chopped finely and combined this way is tasty, and a one pot meal, leaving you lots of time for other things. Try to use a deep casserole pot or a deep sufuria, as it has to be layered.

Ingredients

- 1 cabbage finely chopped, combined with 2 bunches *sukuma wiki* also chopped finely, blanch in boiling water for 5 minutes and then rinse immediately under cold running water
- 2 pkts sausages of your choice, skins removed and each sausage flattened slightly

- ½ cup double cream
- some butter to dot each layer
- salt and pepper to sprinkle lightly on each layer too

Method

- In a deep casserole (oven proof) place a layer of the combined, cabbage-*sukuma wiki* followed by a layer of the sausage meat, dot with butter, salt and pepper and a little cream, continue the layers to the top, finishing off with the cabbage.
- Put a greased, tin foil sheet on top and place the lid firmly on.
- Place in an oven pre-heated to 200°C, for about 35 minutes. Let it rest for about 5 minutes before serving, cut the layers like you would for a lasagne. If you like, you my add a sprinkle of your favourite cheese in between the layers.

Serves 4

· · · · · · · · · · · · · · · · · · · ·

Exotic sautéed carrots

These sweet, nutty carrots are sure to please the fussiest child, or so I hope.

Ingredients

- 6 carrots peeled, sliced and blanched (placed in a bowl with salted boiling water poured over them, for about 7 minutes, drain well
- 40 gm butter
- 4 tbsp honey
- 1 tsp lime juice
- salt and pepper to taste
- ½ cup pistachio (or cashew) nuts crushed

Method

- In a pan over medium heat, melt the butter, adding the carrots and sauté for a few minutes.
- Pour in the honey and lime juice, followed by the nuts, season, let the carrots caramelize a bit and serve right away.
- Top with some chopped parsley for that added effect.

Serves 2

· · · · · · · · · · · · · · · · · · · ·

Aubergine dip

Perfect served with warm bread and relaxing drinks.

Ingredients

- 4 large aubergines, halved
- 1 onion, thinly sliced
- 2 – 3 cloves garlic, crushed
- ½ cup mixed salad oil and olive oil
- juice of 1½ limes
- salt and freshly milled pepper to taste

Method

- Pre-heat oven to about 250°C (gas mark 7).
- Place the aubergines whole in a casserole and bake for 40 minutes.
- Remove from the oven, cool and peel.
- Chop up the aubergines very finely and place in a bowl with salt, pepper, garlic, onion and lime juice. Blend or put through a sieve.
- Mix with a wooden spoon. Gradually add the oil while stirring rapidly. Check seasoning and chill.
- Serve with warm bread.

························

Home-made sweet mango chutney

This is great with curry and cold meat.

Ingredients

- 4 raw mangoes, peeled, de-seeded and thinly sliced
- 1½ cups sugar
- 1 tbsp crushed ginger
- 2 cups wine vinegar
- 2 cardamoms
- 6-8 black peppercorns
- 3 cinnamon sticks
- 1 cup water
- salt, pepper and chilli powder to taste

Method

- In a heavy pan over a low flame, dissolve sugar in water, then add the rest of the ingredients and simmer for about 40 minutes, stirring occasionally. Most of the liquid should have evaporated and you should be left with a pulpy mixture.
- Check the seasoning.
- Once cool, refrigerate in glass bottles.
- Keeps for about 2 weeks.

Cucumber sauté

Ingredients

- 1 kg (2.2 lb) cucumbers peeled, seeded, cut into 'C-shaped' blocks and blanched
- 1 tbsp cream
- 4 tbsp butter
- salt and freshly milled pepper
- parsley to garnish

Method

- Melt the butter in a pan over a medium fire and sauté the cucumbers for about 7 minutes. They should be still firm.
- Add the cream.
- Season and garnish. Ideally, this dish should be prepared just before going to the table.

Serves 4

. . . .

Baked matoke (cooking banans)

Ingredients

- 8 matoke (cooking banans), washed and wrapped in foil (do not peel)

Method

- Pre-heat oven to high. When temperature is reached, reduce heat to medium.
- Place matoke in the oven for about 30 minutes or until done, like sweet potatoes or jacket potatoes.
- Serve hot with butter, salt and pepper.

Note: The skin is not edible.

Serves 4

. . . .

Potatoes dauphinois . . . really yummy

Ingredients

- 1 kg (2.2 lb) potatoes, thinly sliced in rounds and blanched
- 30 g butter
- 1 large clove garlic, crushed
- 180 gm (6½ oz) cheddar cheese, grated

- a little parmesan cheese, grated
- 150 ml (5 fl oz) cream
- 1 egg, beaten
- 300 ml (½ pint) hot milk
- nutmeg
- salt and freshly milled pepper

Method

- Mix the garlic with ½ the butter and rub the baking pan generously with the mixture. Layer the potatoes in the pan until they reach half way up.
- Sprinkle with a little cheese.
- Repeat this process with the remaining potatoes.
- Whisk the egg, milk and nutmeg together in a bowl, warm gently in a pan and stir in salt and pepper.
- Pour this mixture over the potatoes, top with the grated cheese (you can use the cheddar and parmesan together) and a few knobs of butter.
- Bake in a moderate oven for about 50 minutes or until the potatoes are cooked through.
- Brown under the grill.

Serves 4

. . . .

Coleslaw

Ingredients

- 1 medium cabbage, chopped up finely, blanched and cooled
- 2 green peppers, seeded and blanched (optional)
- 2 medium carrots, finely grated
- 2 cups mayonnaise
- 2 stems celery, finely chopped
- lime juice
- salt and pepper

Method

- Mix all the ingredients and season well.
- A little sugar may be added.

Hint: Coleslaw keeps longer (several days) without green pepper and onions. However, if you like the taste of these, you can add them when you are about to serve.

Serves 4

. . . .

Peas

The frozen variety is much better than the pellets normally available.

Ingredients

- 500 gm (1 lb) fresh or frozen peas
- 1 lettuce heart, sliced
- 10 small onions, finely chopped
- 2 tbsp cream
- 4 tbsp butter, plus a little bit extra
- ¼ tbsp mixed herbs
- 1 tbsp sugar
- 1 tbsp salt
- ¼ cup water

Method

- Place the peas, lettuce, onions, herbs, butter, water and seasoning in a pan.
- Bring to a rolling boil and then simmer for about 20 minutes. When the peas are cooked (check water after 10 minutes) drain, add a little more butter and cream.
- Warm through and serve.

Serves 4

. . . .

Ratatouille

Whether served cold or with a roast, this dish is delicious. It's an ideal filling for omelettes, too. Many people throw in all the vegetables and sauté them and then stew them into a messy slush and call this ratatouille. This recipe guarantees optimum results.

Ingredients

- 450 gm (1 lb) courgettes, quartered
- 2 aubergines, sliced, soaked in brine for 10 minutes, drained
- 3 green peppers, sliced, seeded and blanched
- 4 onions, sliced
- 900 gm (2 lb) tomatoes
- 5 cloves garlic, crushed
- ½ cup olive oil (or ½ olive, ½ corn)
- ½ cup dry white wine
- ½ tbsp mixed herbs
- salt and freshly milled pepper

Method

- Heat some of the oil and sauté the tomatoes with the garlic. Simmer. In another pan, briefly sauté the onions and green peppers.
- In a larger pan, add the rest of the oil, the courgettes and eggplant and sauté this.
- Put all the other vegetables in the larger pan and add wine, herbs and seasoning.
- Do not over-cook. This dish can be eaten hot or cold.

Hint: Left-over ratatouille can be topped with a cheese sauce and baked in an oven to recreate a "new" dish.

Serves 4

. . . .

Creamed potatoes

Ingredients

- 1 kg (2.2 lb) boiled potatoes
- 1 cup milk
- 2 tbsp butter
- salt and freshly milled pepper
- parsley

Method

- Put the potatoes through a sieve or blender.
- Place the purée in a heavy pan on low heat.
- Gradually add the milk then butter, stirring all the time. If too thick, add more milk. Season.
- Before serving top with parsley.

Hint: To re-heat, use a bain-marie.

Serves 4

. . . .

Plain rice

Ingredients

- 1 cup rice
- 2½ cups water
- ½ tbsp butter
- salt

Method

- Clean the rice and run under cold water a few times.
- Place the rice with water, salt and butter in a pan over a high flame. Let the water boil then lower heat to an absolute minimum.

- Cover. Leave for about 18 minutes. The rice should be cooked just right. To vary the flavour, you can add one teaspoon of lightly roasted cumin or fried onions. You can also add cooked peas and cashew nuts.

Serves 2

Sautéd tomatoes

Ingredients

- 1 kg (2.2 lb) tomatoes, skinned and cubed
- 6 onions, chopped
- 9 cloves garlic, crushed
- 2 tbsp butter
- ½ cup vegetable oil
- 1 tsp tomato purée
- 1 stock cube dissolved in 1 cup hot water
- a dash of tabasco
- a dash of Worcestershire sauce
- 1 tbsp vinegar
- ½ tsp mixed herbs
- salt and freshly milled pepper

Method

- Fry the onions in the butter and vegetable oil until clear.
- Add the tomatoes, tomato purée and garlic.
- Sauté for about 5 minutes.
- Add the stock, tabasco, Worcestershire sauce, vinegar and herbs. Season according to your taste and heat through. This recipe goes well with fish meuniere or can be used as an accompaniment to a variety of meat dishes.

· · · · · · · · · · · · · · · · · · · ·

Garlic bread

Ingredients

- 1 baguette, sliced in ½ lengthwise
- 6 tsp butter
- 3 cloves garlic, crushed
- 3 tsp fresh parsley, chopped
- a dash of soya sauce mixed with a pinch of pepper

Method

- Mix the butter with the garlic, parsley and soya sauce.
- Spread this mixture on both sides of the bread.
- Replace the two halves of the baguette and wrap with foil.
- Place in a medium oven for 10 minutes.

- Unwrap the baguette and return to the oven for about 4 minutes.
- Serve.

....

Lime chutney

Ingredients

- 8 limes, peeled, de-seeded and sliced
- 5 onions, finely chopped
- 500 ml (17 fl oz) wine vinegar
- 2 cups brown sugar
- ½ tbsp salt
- 2 tbsp mustard seeds
- 10 whole black peppercorns
- 1 tbsp fresh ginger, crushed
- 2 tsp cayenne pepper
- 4 cloves
- 4 – 5 cinnamon sticks

Method

- Mix the limes, onions and salt in a bowl. Leave covered for 24 hours in the refrigerator.
- Using a heavy pan, mix all the ingredients together and gently bring to the boil. Simmer until the lime is tender.
- Remove from the fire and allow it to cool.
- Turn into glass jars and refrigerate until needed. A great accompaniment to curry, cheese and sandwiches, the chutney can keep for up to six weeks.

....

Home-made tomato sauce

Ingredients

- 1 kg (2.2 lb) ripe red tomatoes, peeled and sliced
- 4 onions, chopped
- 3 cloves garlic, crushed
- 2 tsp tomato purée
- 3 tbsp butter
- ½ stock cubes dissolved in ½ cup hot water
- ½ cup dry white wine
- ¼ tsp mixed herbs
- ½ tsp chopped basil
- ½ tsp sugar
- salt and freshly milled pepper
- 2 tsp parsley

Method

- In a heavy pan, fry the onions in the butter over a medium flame until they are light brown.
- Add the tomatoes, garlic and mixed herbs and fry until the tomatoes are tender.
- Add the stock, wine and tomato puree and cook for 15 minutes or until tender.
- Remove from heat and put the mixture through a sieve or blender and add the seasoning together with the sugar, parsley and basil.

. . . .

Herb mayonnaise

You can use herbs of your choice.

Ingredients

- 2 cups mayonnaise
- 2½ tbsp chives, chopped
- 1 tbsp onions, chopped
- 1 tsp mixed herbs
- 1 clove garlic

Method

- Mix all the ingredients well.

Hint: Freshly-made mayonnaise will keep in the refrigerator for only 3 days; the safest policy is to make it when you need it.

. . . .

Hot pepper sauce

Beware, this is a lethal weapon! But it tastes amazingly nice and is different from the usual chili sauce.

Ingredients

- 1 gm (8 oz) small red chillies
- 2 tsp salt
- dry sherry

Method

- Wash the chillies and lay them on a tray to dry a little in the sun. Do not allow them to become completely dry.
- Meanwhile, clean and dry an old jam jar.
- Put the chillies into it together with the salt.
- Fill the jar with the sherry.
- Refrigerate. Use the sauce after a month when needed.
- When the sherry is used up, you can top it up a few times.

Yoghurt chutney

Ingredients

- 1½ cups yoghurt
- 2 bunches mint, finely chopped
- 1 bunch dhania, finely chopped
- ½ tsp salt
- ¼ tsp sugar
- chillies to taste

Method

- Mix all the ingredients together.
- Chill.

Hint: Keep the chutney refrigerated. It should keep for up to 4 days.

. . . .

Pancakes

Choose a day when you do not have much to do and therefore have the patience to stand in front of the cooker swirling batter endlessly around the pan.

Ingredients

- 2 cups flour
- 1¾ cups milk
- ¼ tsp salt for savoury pancakes *or* 1½ tsp sugar for sweet
- 3 eggs, beaten
- butter for frying (you will need about 2 tsp per pancake) done well
- salted water

Method

- Mix the flour and salt or sugar, depending on whether you want sweet or savoury pancakes.
- Gradually whisk in the milk and eggs, blending smoothly to avoid lumps. If it is slightly lumpy, put the mixture through a medium sieve to get rid of them. Let the mixture stand for at least 1½ hours.
- Heat the pan and add a little butter. When hot, over a medium flame add about 2 tbsp of the batter and "swirl" the pan to spread it.
- After about 1 minute turn the pancake and cook the other side, adding a little butter to the side of the pan as it cooks. Continue until the butter is finished.

Serving suggestions: *Savoury pancakes can be filled with creamed spinach or sautéed mushrooms with cream or cheese sauce for a delicious main meal. Sweet pancakes can be filled with fresh fruit sprinkled with icing sugar, served with* *cream on the side. With a little bit of creativity, you can come up with your special fillings. Wrapped in foil, pancakes freeze well and can last up to 3 months.*

. . . .

Asparagus with butter or vinaigrette

Try to find asparagus that is not too "husky" at the stems.

Ingredients

- 1 bunch asparagus
- 4 tbsp butter
- ½ bunch parsley, chopped
- salt and pepper
- water

Method

- Wash the asparagus well. Cut off the tough stems and peel the fibrous bits.
- Alternatively, cut four inches beneath the tip and use the hard bits for a delicious soup. Plunge into boiling water with a little salt for 15 minutes or until tender.
- Warm the butter and add parsley. Lay the asparagus onto a warmed platter, pour some butter over it and sprinkle with a little milled pepper.
- Substitute the butter with vinaigrette sauce for a different taste.

Serves 4

. . . .

Artichokes

Ingredients

- 4 artichokes, washed well
- salted water

Method

- Boil the artichokes for about 15 minutes or until the leaves come out easily.
- Serve with hot butter (see the recipe for asparagus). Do not discard the heart, as many do. It is edible as long as you clear the fibrous spikes first, using your fingers.

Serves 4

. . . .

Potato fritters

Ingredients

- 8 medium potatoes, skinned and grated
- 3 onions, grated
- 2 eggs, beaten
- parsley, chopped
- plain flour
- oil for deep-frying
- a dash of Worcestershire sauce
- salt and pepper

Method

- Mix all the ingredients together except the flour. When the potatoes are well coated in the mixture, roll them in the flour.
- Mould into small patties and fry in the oil over a medium flame until both sides are medium brown.
- Turn onto a platter.

Hint: You can also mix in a clove of crushed garlic or ½ a bunch of chopped dhania or green chilli according to your taste.

Serves 4

· · · · · · · · · · · · · · · · · · · ·

Mushroom omelette

I prefer to use field mushrooms for this recipe as they taste delicious. However, you may not always find them, in which case use button, oyster or shiitake mushrooms. Do not accept field mushrooms under any circumstances without making sure that they are safe. Some greengrocers occasionally have them, so if you can get them from a reliable source, try them.

Ingredients

- 1 punnet mushrooms, soaked for 5 minutes in a little water with vinegar
- drain and rinse
- 8 eggs, beaten
- ½ cup milk
- 3 tbsp butter
- parsley, chopped
- salt and pepper

Method

- Melt butter in a large heavy pan and sauté the mushrooms with salt, pepper and parsley for at least 8 minutes.

- Turn the grill on to full.
- Mix the milk with beaten eggs and gradually add to the mushrooms.
- Alternate the cooking from the stove to the grill. This requires quite a bit of skill, and ensures that there is no turning required. If you can master this, the omelette will be beautifully fluffy and you have absolute control over how well it is, according to your preference.
- Serve with bread.

Serves 4

· · · · · · · · · · · · · · · · · · · ·

Cheese soufflé

Soufflés are not as difficult to make as many people imagine. Just avoid the temptation to open the oven before time, not even for a "peep". A soufflé is a welcome change and light too!

Ingredients

- 125 gm (4 oz) butter
- plain flour
- 1 cup cheddar cheese, grated
- 1 cup milk
- 4 eggs separated; beat the yolks and put aside the whites
- 1 extra egg white
- ¼ tsp mixed herbs
- pepper

Method

- Lightly grease a baking dish with butter. Turn on the oven to medium high.
- In a heavy pan over low heat, melt the butter and add the flour. Stir for 1 minute.
- Remove the pan from the heat and gradually add the milk.
- Return the pan to the fire, still on low heat, and stir constantly.
- The mixture will thicken after a few minutes. Still stirring, add the pepper, cheese and mixed herbs. Heat through but do not allow the sauce to boil.
- Remove from the fire and put the mixture in a bowl. Stir in the egg yolks. Whisk all the egg whites until they are firm. Fold gently into the cheese mixture without stirring. Spoon into the baking dish and bake in the oven for 25 minutes. The soufflé is ready when it turns golden brown.
- Serve immediately

· · · · · · · · · · · · · · · · · · · ·

Arrow-root with cheese

A vegetable with a difference. You may add other vegetables of your choice to this versatile dish.

- 1 kg 2.2 lb arrow-roots, washed well
- 2½ tbsp corn flour
- 4 tbsp butter
- 1 onion, finely chopped
- 500 ml (16 oz) milk
- ¾ cup cheddar cheese, grated
- 1 tbsp brandy
- ½ cup white wine vinegar or malt vinegar
- parmesan cheese
- breadcrumbs
- salt and pepper to taste

Method

- Place the arrow-roots in a pan of boiling water with a little salt and vinegar and boil for 25 minutes or until tender.
- Remove, allow to cool, then peel and cut into slices. Place in a bowl of water with a little vinegar.
- Melt the butter in another pan, add the onion and fry for 1 minute. Lower the heat, and then gradually add the corn flour, little at a time. Add the milk, stirring all the time to prevent lumps from forming, and then pour in the brandy. The mixture should thicken as it heats up.
- Mix in the grated cheddar cheese and season. Do not allow the sauce to boil.
- Place the arrow-root in a buttered casserole, pour the cheese sauce over it and sprinkle breadcrumbs and parmesan cheese to cover the surface of the sauce.
- Bake in a moderate oven for 20 minutes.
- Place the casserole under the grill to brown.

Serves 4

· · · · · · · · · · · · · · · · · · · ·

Mushrooms with dry sherry

Ingredients

- 1 punnet mushrooms, washed and soaked in a little water with vinegar
- 3 tbsp butter
- 8 tbsp dry sherry
- ½ tsp mixed herbs
- 1 clove garlic, crushed
- a little fresh parsley to garnish
- a dash of cream (optional)
- salt and freshly ground pepper

Method

- Finely slice the mushrooms and sauté in the butter and garlic for a few minutes. Add the sherry and mixed herbs.
- Allow the liquid to reduce a little.
- Season with the salt and pepper; add a dash of cream if liked. If you use cream, heat through but do not allow to boil.
- Sprinkle with chopped parsley when ready to serve.

· ·

Cucumbers with mint and cream

Ingredients

- 6 cucumbers, peeled (slice in ½ lengthwise, scoop out the seeds with a teaspoon and slice)
- 3 tbsp butter
- 1 tbsp fresh mint
- ½ tsp corn flour
- 1 cup fresh cream
- a little milk (optional)
- salt and pepper to taste

Method

- Sauté the cucumbers in the butter for about 5 minutes.
- Meanwhile, mix the cream with the corn flour and add to the cucumbers with the mint.
- Allow to simmer for about 4 minutes. Season according to taste. If the sauce gets too thick, add some milk.

Serves 4

· ·

Chapter 8

Pasta and other Italian dishes

Fresh pasta sauce

Simply heat the olive oil just when the pasta is cooked and add the rest of the ingredients to this hot but **not** *smoking oil. Serve with a salad, dressing follows.*

Ingredients

- ¼ cup extra virgin olive oil (put this in a pan ready to heat)
- 3 tbsp basil chopped
- 1 tbsp fresh thyme
- 2 tbsp fresh parsley
- 1 tbsp fresh chives chopped
- 8 lightly roasted cashews finely pounded
- 2 cloves garlic
- 1 tbsp lime /lemon juice
- salt and pepper to taste
- grated parmesan to be added to the finished dish

Method

- When your pasta is cooked, heat the olive oil and add all the ingredients, *except* the parmesan. Do not let the oil smoke, and remove from heat almost immediately after adding the ingredients.
- Mix with the pasta, serve onto warmed plates, sprinkle the parmesan lavishly and enjoy.
- Serve with a crisp green salad with a dressing of your choice and good french bread.

Dressing, for the salad:
- 3 cloves garlic crushed
- ⅓ cup extra virgin olive oil
- 2 tbsp red wine vinegar
- ½ a tsp dried mixed herbs

- 4 tbsp thick Greek yoghurt or put in muslin cloth and let it drip for an hour before use
- 2 tbsp mayonnaise
- salt and pepper to taste

Method
- Mix well, and add to your salad just when needed.

Serves 4

. . . .

Haraka haraka spaghetti

A quick version of the famous tomato sauce spaghetti that we all once loved ... with a few added ingredients to pep it up further. For the sauce, place in a blender.

Ingredients

- 5 cloves garlic
- 18 sundried tomato pieces, oil drained
- handful of olives pitted
- 130 ml extra virgin olive oil
- 3 large tomatoes, seeded
- I tsp sugar
- 3 tbsp capers
- dash tabasco
- 1 bunch chopped basil, tear by hand
- a ¼ tsp mixed herbs
- salt and pepper to taste

Method
- Whizz until smooth. To add at the end ... a good sprinkle of parmesan cheese over the pasta and chopped parsley, 360 g spaghetti, cooked as per instructions.
- Heat the sauce in an extra large pan, when hot and thick (add some tomato puree if too thin). Taste and correct seasoning.
- Mix the pasta in, heat through, serve on warmed plates, topped with the parmesan and chopped parsley. Sometimes as a variation, add a can or two of plain, drained tuna, to the sauce and omit the cheese.
- Serve with a green salad and some crusty bread.

Serves 4

. . . .

Spaghetti puttanesca

A warming, simple sauce full of flavour and delicious.

Ingredients

- 5 tbsp extra virgin olive oil
- 4 cloves garlic crushed
- 2 onions finely chopped
- 1 small red chilli
- 1 can anchovies in olive oil drained, chopped
- 450 gm canned tomatoes (add more if you like)
- ½ tsp dried oregano
- 100 gm black olives pitted and quartered
- 1 tbsp capers, (salted) washed
- season with salt and pepper
- 1 bunch parsley, chopped to add at the end
- 400 gm spaghetti, cooked according to instructions on pack, once the sauce is ready

Method

- Heat the olive oil on a medium flame and add the garlic, onions and chilli. Sauté for a little while, add the anchovies, tomatoes and oregano.
- Reduce the heat and let simmer until sauce thickens, adding the olives and capers.
- Season according to taste.
- Warm your plates, mix the sauce with the spaghetti and top with parsley, serve at once. Quite addictive.

Serves 4

· · · · · · · · · · · · · · · · · · · ·

Spaghetti with garlic, olive oil and chilli

A rather quick pasta dish that requires no time and ingredients that most households would have. It is tasty too – serve alongside some warmed crusty bread ⟨…⟩aven.

Ingredients

- 250 gm spaghetti
- 6 tbsp extra virgin olive oil
- 4 cloves garlic, crushed
- 1 red or even green chilli de seeded and chopped very fine
- freshly milled pepper and a little salt
- parsley to finish off

Method

- Cook the pasta according to instructions not forgetting to add salt.
- Heat the olive oil gently and add the garlic, chilli, black pepper, salt (little … you can add more later). When the pasta is *al dente* – just firm to the teeth – drain and add the olive oil mix.
- Serve on warmed plates. Dot with parsley.
- Though not really done traditionally, you may sprinkle some parmesan if liked and use ½ olive oil and the rest butter. Rich it will be. Have also some crispy salad on the side and there you are.

Serves 2

· · · · · · · · · · · · · · · · · · · ·

Linguine with gorgonzola sauce

This is a good strong flavoured sauce. If gorgonzola is not available use good local blue cheese, which is quite acceptable though a bit milder in taste.

Ingredients

- 500 gm dried linguine cooked according to instructions on pack
  Meanwhile . . .
  In a pan over medium heat, add and bring almost to the boil:
- 350 ml double cream, remove from heat and add
- 350 gorgonzola (small cubes)
- add the cooked pasta to this

Method

- Season salt and pepper according to taste, serve on warmed plates, with crisp crusty bread and you are in heaven.

Serves 4

· · · · · · · · · · · · · · · · · · · ·

Pasta with parmesan and gruyere

A soothing quick pasta dish. I use tagliatelle, but you can substitute with other dried pasta that is thin.

Ingredients

- cook 500 gm pasta as per instructions on pack
  When cooked drain and add to the pasta
- 4 tbsp good olive oil
- 50 gm gruyere cheese
- 110 gm freshly grated parmesan
- salt and pepper to season
- a few chopped seeded tomatoes to decorate

Method

- Serve on warmed plates, with the tomatoes scattered around. If you cannot find gruyere, you may use any other cheese as a substitute, though the taste will be altered. I have found that at times a compromise is better than nothing! Enjoy.

Serves 4

....

Fettuccine alfredo

A quick ready to go pasta dish. If fettuccine is not available use what is available (tagliatelle etc)

Ingredients

In a large pot, bring to boil:
- 7 l water
- 2½ tbsp salt
Then add 500 gm pasta and cook till just under done a little. Drain and drizzle a little olive oil over and mix. Set aside.
In a large pan, melt:
- 125 gm butter, *lower heat and add:*
- 1 clove crushed garlic (optional)
- 260 gm double cream
- 80 gm freshly grated parmesan cheese
- salt and pepper to taste
- chopped parsley to top the pasta

Method

- Mix in the cooked pasta and heat through, over low heat. It should be just *al dente.*
- Check seasoning and serve on warmed plates, sprinkle over with parsley.
- I think you will like the idea that this dish in particular can be prepared so easily and quickly. Ideal when a friend just drops in or you have had hectic day.

Serves 4

....

Pesto

A fine sauce easily made, to mix with your favourite pasta or ravioli. Freshly made it puts to shame all the bottled varieties. Make it in quantity, freeze it and it is as good as it was when you first made it. If you do not have a food processor, then you will have to use a mortar and pestle. In a food processor place:

Ingredients

- 160 ml extra virgin olive oil
- 4 cloves of garlic
- 2 cups fresh Basil leaves
- ½ cup pine nuts (or hazel nuts)
- 5 tbsp grated parmesan (or pecorino)

Method

- Whizz (or pound) as best as you can and then drizzle steadily 160 ml extra virgin olive oil until you get a fairly fine paste. Sometimes I leave it a little course to get extra texture.
- Season with a little salt and pepper. This will make about 1 cup of pesto, enough for about 400 gm pasta or ravioli.
- Before adding the pesto, leave about a tbsp of the water from the cooked pasta, to mix with the pesto…it makes it much easier to mix.
- Top with a little more parmesan cheese and, hey you have a feast fit for a king. Some crusty bread is about else you need.

Serves 3 – 4

. . . .

Mediterranean pasta

Pasta that is light, fruity and can be eaten hot or at room temperature. This one in particular is again quick but equally irresistible. Kenya has some wonderful canned tuna, try it.

Ingredients

- 500 gm pasta of your choice, cooked, according to the instructions on the pack; be sure its *al dente*
  In a large bow mix:
- 20 black olive (pitted and chopped)
- 3 tbsp pine nuts or walnuts, toasted and chopped
- 2 bunches fresh basil, chopped
- 3 cans tuna (about 160 gm per can) drained
- 2 cloves garlic crushed
- 4 tbsp parsley chopped
- juice of 1 lemon
- 7 tbsp extra virgin olive oil
- salt and pepper to taste

Method

- Add the above to the drained pasta, serve warm or at room temperature, with some lovely chilled wine. A casual, unpretentious meal, warming to the heart and soul.

Serves 4

Sun dried tomato pesto

We have a good range of local sun dried tomatoes which are perfectly good and inexpensive. Use pasta of your choice. The thin stringy varieties are better. The flavour of this pesto is one of concentrated tomato. Rather nice and heart warming after a hard day. Place in a food processor.

Ingredients

- 230 gm moist sun tomatoes (drain oil...)
- 2 clove garlic
- ½ spoon chilli pepper flakes (or just cut one small red chilli pepper)
- 5 tbsp extra virgin olive oil
- salt and pepper to taste
  Whizz this till smooth, set aside.
- 480 gm pasta of your choice

Method

- Cook the pasta according to the instructions on pack, until *al dente*, mix with the pesto, check seasoning and correct if needed, top with grated parmesan cheese, serve on warmed plates, with some rocket or a salad of your choice. Amazingly simple, quick to make and ever so hearty to eat.

Serves 4

....

Aubergine and courgette salad

A light and lovely vegetarian dish, for those times when you want a change.

Ingredients

- 8 medium-sized aubergines, thinly sliced and soaked in brine for 20 minutes and then drained
- 14 courgettes, thinly sliced lengthwise
- 8 – 10 almonds, blanched and crushed
- 1 cup oil (mix ½ virgin olive, ½ good vegetable oil)
- lime juice
- 6 cloves garlic, crushed (mix with oil)
- 1 tsp sesame seeds, lightly roasted
- crisp lettuce, carefully washed
- salt and freshly milled pepper to taste

Method

- Line a large platter with the lettuce leaves.
- Set the grill between medium to full.

- Lay out the sliced aubergines and courgettes on the grill rack. Mix the oil with the crushed garlic, sesame seeds and lime juice.
- Brush the aubergines and courgettes with the oil and garlic mixture.
- Grill until each side is light brown colour, making sure that you keep on brushing more of the oil and garlic to prevent the vegetables from drying out.
- Once the vegetables are done, lay them on the lettuce-lined platter.
- Sprinkle a little salt and pepper according to taste.
- Garnish with the crushed almonds.

Serves 4 – 6

· · · · · · · · · · · · · · · · · · · ·

Nutty chicken salad with sesame seeds

The combination of pine nuts and sesame seeds will drive you ... nuts!

Ingredients

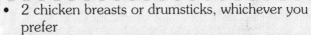

- 2 chicken breasts or drumsticks, whichever you prefer
- 4 tbsp sesame seeds, lightly roasted
- 6 tbsp pine nuts or almonds, blanched, skinned, roasted lightly and finely chopped
- 1 lettuce washed very carefully with salt water; use only the crisp inner bits and shred
- ½ bunch spring onions, chopped
- 1 cucumber, peeled, seeded and finely sliced
- 2 tomatoes, washed, seeded and sliced
- 4 artichoke hearts or asparagus tips, cooked
- 2 eggs, boiled, sliced and sprinkled with a little lime juice
- 1 chicken stock cube dissolved in 1 cup hot water
- 2 cups white wine
- ½ tsp mixed herbs

Method

- Poach the chicken with the stock cube, water, white wine and mixed herbs. When tender cut into thin strips.
- Mix in all the nuts, sesame seeds, lettuce, lions, cucumber and tomatoes in a glass bowl. Then decorate the salad with eggs and artichoke hearts or asparagus tips.

For the dressing, use either vinaigrette or mix the following ingredients together:

- 4 tbsp mayonnaise
- 2 tbsp tomato ketchup

- 1 tbsp brandy
- juice of ½ a lime
- a dash of Worcestershire sauce
- 2 cloves of garlic, crushed
- ½ tsp fresh ginger, crushed (optional)
- a little wine vinegar
- salt and freshly milled pepper

Hint: The seasoning should be added according to your taste.

Serves 4

· ·

Macaroni cheese with tomato and tuna

This is quite a pleasant combination. You can use any variety of pasta apart from macaroni to vary this dish.

Ingredients

- 1 tin tuna fish, drained
- 2 onions, finely chopped
- 2 cloves garlic, crushed
- 6 fresh tomatoes, skinned and chopped
- 3 tbsp butter
- 2½ tbsp corn flour
- 570 ml (1 pint) milk
- 115 gm cheddar, grated
- 2 tbsp breadcrumbs
- salt and freshly milled pepper

Method

- Cook the macaroni according to the manufacturer's instructions. In a heavy pan over a medium flame, fry the onions in the butter until clear.
- Add the tomatoes and garlic and fry for about 7 minutes. Lower the heat.
- Mix the milk with the corn flour and add slowly to the pan, stirring all the time.
- The mixture should be quite thick. If it is not, add a little more corn flour mixed with water.
- Add the cheese and lower the heat further.
- Place the tuna fish in the pan with the seasoning.
- Mix the sauce with the macaroni gently and pour into a greased casserole dish.
- Sprinkle with breadcrumbs and place in a pre-heated oven on medium heat for about ½ an hour. Brown under grill if necessary.

Hint: If your mixture becomes lumpy by mistake, do not panic! Simply put it through a sieve.

Serves 4

Spaghetti bolognese

Ingredients

- 1 kg (2.2 lb) minced beef
- 8 potatoes, peeled and chopped
- 3 onions, finely sliced
- 4 cloves garlic, crushed
- 2 tbsp tomato purée
- 2 tbsp oil (mix olive and corn oil)
- ¾ cup dry white wine
- 2 stock cubes dissolved in 1 cup hot water
- ½ tsp mixed herbs
- black pepper
- ¾ cup equal portions cheddar and parmesan cheese, grated
- 250 gm (8 oz) spaghetti cooked according to instructions on pack

Method

- Heat the oil in a heavy pan over a medium flame, sauté the onions; add garlic and mince, stirring all the time. The mince should cook until it is well browned and there is no liquid left.
- Add the tomatoes and mix well for about 2 minutes. Stir in the wine, stock, tomato puree, black pepper and herbs.
- Allow to simmer for an hour.
- Serve with spaghetti, cheese on the side and a salad of your choice.

Serves 6

. . . .

Pasta salad

This is a quick, simple but delicious salad that can be served as a main meal.

Ingredients

- ½ packet pasta (any variety except spaghetti)
For the marinade:
- ½ cup olive oil
- ½ cup lime juice
- 2 cloves garlic, crushed
- 2 medium tomatoes, seeded and quartered
- salt and freshly milled pepper
- 1 bunch parsley, chopped
- ½ bunch asparagus, cooked
- 8 artichoke hearts
- 1 medium onion, finely chopped

- 2 – 3 tbsp parmesan cheese, grated
- ½ punnet raw mushrooms, sliced
- 4 thin slices ham, diced
- 10 – 15 black olives, pitted
- ½ bunch dhania, chopped, to garnish

Method

- Mix the ingredients for the marinade and correct the seasoning. Let it sit for about 15 minutes.
- Cook the pasta according to the manufacturer's instructions and mix it in with the marinade. This salad can be served warm or cold. If you prefer it warm, once you drain the pasta mix it in immediately.
- Serve with warm garlic bread.

Serves 4

· ·

![Chapter 9]

Adil's home-made hints

Easy chicken stock

Ingredients

- 1 kg (2.2 lb) chicken bones, washed
- 2 medium onions, chopped
- 1 medium carrot, chopped
- 2 sticks celery, chopped
- 1 tbsp mixed herbs
- 6 pepper corns
- 1 tbsp butter
- 1 tbsp oil
- 1 l water

Method

- Fry the celery, onions and chicken bones in the oil over a medium flame for about 4 minutes then add water, vegetables, pepper corns and herbs and bring to a comfortable boil for an hour. Skim.
- Strain the stock and skim off the fat.
- Refrigerated, it will keep for only 2 – 3 days. So try to either freeze it or make your stock fresh each time you need to use it. It is so much nicer.

. . . .

Vegetable stock

Especially convenient for strict vegetarians, this stock can be added to stews and soups, for example corn soup or mixed vegetable soup.

Ingredients

- 4 carrots, washed and scrubbed
- 3 onions, chopped
- 7 celery sticks
- 2 parsnips
- 4 bay leaves
- 3 l (12 cups) water

Method

- Mix all the ingredients together, bring to the boil then simmer for about 1½ hours.
- Skim often. Strain. This stock freezes well.

·····················

Home-made yoghurt

I find it strange that in Kenya, where people use yoghurt for so many things, they buy it from the shops. If you have the money, I guess there is nothing wrong with that, but yoghurt made at home is so much tastier. Getting the starter is usually the hardest part, but if you have any Indian friends, they are bound to have some. You only need 3 tbsp of their yoghurt – that is your starter. Then, each time you make some yoghurt, reserve a little of the starter for your next lot. There is an old story about making yoghurt at home. I have always wondered if it is true, but perhaps you should test it and see: according to the story, if it works you are in love! So here goes . . . but try it in small quantities first, until you get the hang of it.

Ingredients

- ½ l (17.5 fl oz) normal milk
- ½ l (17.5 fl oz) UHT milk
- 3 tbsp "starter"

Method

- Mix the two types of milk and boil. Allow it to cool, but not to reach room temperature. When it reaches about blood temperature, whisk in the starter.
- Leave overnight in a warm place. (An oven switched on for about 5 minutes and then switched off is good enough. Alternatively, stand it in the cupboard where your hot water tank is). Hope it works! Yoghurt can be used as a drink by adding cool water, salt, pepper and cumin seeds then whisking it.
- For most of the recipes that require the use of cream, you can safely substitute it with yoghurt mixed with corn flour (about 2 tsp to ½ l yoghurt to prevent curdling.

Things you can do with yoghurt
- Yoghurt is a wonderful marinade for steaks and chicken, mixed with herbs and spices of your choice.
- Marinate for at least 8 – 12 hours in the refrigerator.
- You can make a delicious mint sauce by simply mixing a bunch of finely chopped mint leaves with a cup of yoghurt.
- Add salt and sugar according to your taste. You can also add a little yoghurt to your salads – it is especially tempting with cucumber and thinly sliced raw onions (optional) and seasoning. Or try it with your own choice of fruit sliced thinly. The best part is: yoghurt is not so heavy on your hips!

·····················

Chapter 10

Desserts

Pancakes

Whether you fill them with creamed spinach, asparagus, or strawberries sprinkled with icing sugar, these are great as a treat and at parties too.

Ingredients

- 1½ cup milk
- 3 eggs
- 1½ cup flour
- ½ tsp salt
- 2 tbsp margarine or butter
- pinch baking powder

Method

- Mix the ingredients in a food processor or even by hand, adding the milk in this case gradually to avoid lumps.
- Grease a non-stick pan lightly and pour thin layers 'rotating' the pan slightly to get an even coat. Heat through and when little spots appear, turn over and then cook other side.
- Place in some foil and keep warm till they are all done. Fill with what you like as I mentioned earlier or even a nice sprinkle of fresh ripe chopped tomatoes, seasoned well with salt and pepper, topped with some good melting type cheese. Have fun.

Serves 2

. . . .

Kenyan trifle

Using passion fruit and double cream, this is very different from the usual trifle.

Ingredients

- 80 gm sponge cake, broken into squares
- 14 digestive biscuits broken into rough halves
- 100 ml medium sherry
- 40 ml brandy
- 400 gm passion fruit, pulp removed and sweetened with sugar from 1 cup upwards according to taste

- extra passion fruit for decoration
- 600 ml double cream, sweetened with 5 tbsp sugar and whipped (again sugar can be adjusted to your taste)

Method

- Place the sponge and biscuits into a serving bowl and sprinkle with the sherry and brandy, pour the passion fruit over and let it get absorbed, then pour the cream over.
- Decorate with the extra passion fruit kind of dribbled over the top, chill and serve. You could also make an extra layer with shop bought custard, jam or even jelly. I have given the basic recipe and you may change it to suit your taste.
- Chill well and serve with extra strong Kenya coffee alongside.

Serves 4

. . . .

Pineapples on fire

A simple dessert, all you need is good Italian ice cream to complement, I have slightly modified this recipe, making it richer.

Ingredients

- 1 ripe pineapple, peeled, cored and sliced
- 5 tbsp brown sugar
- 3 – 4 tbsp unsalted butter
- 10 tbsp brandy
- ½ cup raisins soaked in water
- ½ cup cashews, roasted and crushed slightly

Method

- Brown the pineapple (both sides) with the butter in a heavy pan over a medium heat. In a smaller pan warm the brandy through. Meanwhile, add the sugar to the pineapple, as soon as it dissolves, pour the brandy over the pineapple, and flame
- Add the raisins and cashews. You may like to cut the pineapple into segments.
- Cool a little and serve with vanilla ice cream. If you need more portions simply double the ingredients.

Serves 2

. . . .

Passion fruit rice pudding

A truly East African twist to the normal rice pudding we know.

Ingredients

- 1 kg passion fruit, washed, sliced in ½ and the pulp removed and put through a sieve. Reserve this liquor for later, sweeten with up to 2 cups of sugar (according to taste or add sweetener)
For the rice pudding:
- 3½ cups milk
- 4 drops real vanilla essence
- 2 tbsp sugar
- ⅓ cup rice

Method

- Combine these ingredients and let them rest for 45 minutes.
- Place in an oven proof dish and add little cubes of unsalted butter on top, cover with foil bake in a moderate oven (180°C) for an hour. Stir every nalf an hour.
- Continue to bake, uncovered for another hour or so till the rice is creamy and soft
- Serve hot or cold with the passion liquor on the side, or dribbled majestically.

Serves 2

. . . .

Mango fool

This desert was ever popular in Kenya in the late 60's and early 70's. It died a sudden death and I would like to see it back again. So many oldie dishes had a similar fate, like beef stroganoff, prawn cocktail, fondue ... they are all coming back. I am glad to say with the phasing out of art on a plate, with towering food, and droppings of basalmic.

Ingredients

- 5 large ripe mangoes peeled
- 3 tbsp water
- juice of 1 lime
- 3 tbsp icing sugar (more if you like it extra sweet)
- good pinch cinnamon
- 1 cup double cream, whipped
- a few chopped pistachio nuts, chopped to top the fool

Method

- In a pan, over a medium heat, place the mangoes in a pan with the water, cover and simmer for about 10 minutes, peek and see ½ way if there is still some water, otherwise add some, cover.
- Remove when soft and with a knife remove the pulp, put it into a food processor, or sieve.

- Add the lime juice, icing sugar, cinnamon.
- Mix this well till sugar is dissolved, taste and check if it is up to pare. Fold in the cream gradually, place in small bowls or one large one, top with the chopped nuts and refrigerate till very cold. Serve. Truly Kenyan.

Serves 4

• •

Deep fried fruit

An unusual way of eating fruit, quite popular with adults and children alike.

Ingredients

- 2 large apples or pears, peeled, cored and coated with some lemon juice to prevent browning
- oil for deep frying
- 3 tbsp icing sugar
- 2 tsp cinnamon
- ice cream to serve with
  The batter:
- 250 gm corn flour
- 250 gm plain flour
- 1 egg
- 1 tsp baking powder
- good pinch salt

Method

- To start with make the batter. Sift the flours and baking powder. Add the egg and some cold water to make a thin batter (not too thin, it should coat the spoon comfortably).
- Place in the refrigerator for 30 minutes.
- Heat the oil. When hot enough, drop a piece of bread that should brown within a minute. Coat each piece of fruit and drop gently into the oil. Do this in batches whilst you keep the done batches warm in a moderately hot oven. When they are all done, place the icing sugar and cinnamon in a sieve, and coat the battered fruit.
- Serve with ice cream of your choice.
- Top your ice cream with some double cream, or melted chocolate. Now that is heaven.

Serves 2

• •

Caramelised grapes

You may use other fruit like soft pears, apples etc. This simple but exciting dessert is well worth a try.

Ingredients

- 2 bunches seedless grapes halved (or then deseed them please)
- 1 wine glass brandy
- 1 carton double cream whipped
- enough soft brown sugar to cover the cream at the end

Method

- Mix the grapes with the brandy and place in a cake baking tin…add the whipped cream thickly on top, mixing the brandy in too.
- Cover fairly well with the brown sugar (according to how sweet you like it). Place in the freezer, till frozen, when ready to eat, put under a grill that is on (full power! until the brown sugar melts and browns further a bit.
- Remove, and serve. You may cover the exterior of the tin with some foil to make it look neater. Serve with good Italian ice cream.

Serves 4

. . . .

Chocolate mousse

Ingredients

- 280 gm (9 oz) dark chocolate
- 4 eggs, separated
- 2 tbsp brandy
- 9 gm (3 oz) cream, whipped
- extra cream for topping
- mint leaves to garnish

Method

- Melt the chocolate pieces in a double boiler.*
- While still on the fire, gradually mix in the egg yolks and brandy. When the mixture begins to thicken, remove from heat and allow to cool.
- Stir in the cream.
- Put the egg whites in a separate bowl and beat until they form stiff white peaks. Fold the whites into the chocolate mixture.
- Spoon into large wine glasses and refrigerate. Before serving, top with whipped cream and garnish with mint leaves.

A double boiler is the same as a bain-marie. Another way of melting the chocolate is to place a large pan of water on medium heat and put a smaller pan containing the chocolate pieces in the hot water.

. . . .

Almond ice cream

This glorious-tasting ice cream can be made with a vanilla or coffee flavour – take your pick.

Ingredients

- 250 ml (9 fl oz) heavy fresh cream, whipped
- 5 tbsp icing sugar
- 1 tsp vanilla essence (or 2 tbsp instant coffee and 1 tbsp rum)
- 3 egg whites
- ¾ cup almonds, blanched for 5 minutes, peeled, dried and finely chopped in a coffee grinder
- extra cream

Method

- Whip the egg whites until they form stiff peaks. Keep aside.
- Mix the whipped cream with the sugar and vanilla essence or coffee with rum. Fold in the egg whites and almonds. Freeze.
- Before serving, remove the ice cream from the freezer and let it thaw a little. Add a little cream, mix well and return to the freezer for 20 minutes. When serving, add a tot of *crème de menthe,* drambuie or Kenya gold liqueur.

Hint: Reserve the egg yolks to make mayonnaise or omelettes.

. . . .

Pears in wine

Ingredients

- 6 pears, peeled, seeded and halved
- 185 gm (6 oz) sugar
- 4 cloves
- 2 sticks cinnamon
- 1 tsp ginger, crushed (optional)
- 3 cups red wine
- juice of 1 lime
- 2 cups water

Method

- Put the water in a pan and over low heat, dissolve the sugar. Add the cloves, cinnamon, lime juice, ginger and pears.

- Cover and simmer for 20 minutes, making sure the liquid does not evaporate completely. Add a little more water if needed.
- Pour in the wine and continue to simmer for 15 minutes. The pears should be tender. If the syrup is not thick enough, remove the pears and reduce the liquid. Remove the pan from the fire, turn the pears into a bowl and chill.

Hint: You can try this with prunes, plums, peaches, cape tomatoes and other fruits.

· ·

Creamed rice pudding

Ingredients

- 1 cup rice, cleaned
- ½ cup cream, whipped
- 2½ cups (20 fl oz) milk
- ½ cup sherry
- ½ cup water
- 3 tbsp sugar
- ½ cup almonds, blanched, peeled and chopped
- ½ cup sultanas, soaked in water
- a pinch of saffron
- cardamom

Method

- Place the milk, water and rice in a heavy pan and bring to the boil. Stir at lower heat and add the sugar, saffron and cardamom. Cover and cook for 20 minutes on very low heat. When cool, put in the sherry and sultanas and fold in the whipped cream.
- Chill and serve.

The chef shares some tips on jelly:
- Add fresh fruit juice instead of water to the jelly powder and a little fruit of your choice.

· ·

Fruit salad

Add fresh orange juice, passion fruit juice and a dash of rum to enhance the fruit flavour. Strawberries: wash, pour a little red wine over them, sprinkle with icing sugar and top with cream. Ice cream: melt chocolate in a double boiler, cool a little and pour over it. Or mix in crushed nuts or cherries, whatever you fancy.

Chapter 11

Drinks

Kenyan passion

Probably the name says it all; there is no fruit as versatile and so remarkably bursting with nature's exotic flavours like the passion fruit.

Ingredients

- 10 passion fruit, cut in ½ and contents removed with spoon and placed in a bowl
- 3 tbsp honey
- ½ cup water
- 2 tsp gelatine or leaf gelatine (equivalent of)
- 1 cup double cream whipped

Method

- Over a low heat in a pan, dissolve the honey in the water stirring all the time, add the gelatine and make sure it too dissolves, add the passion fruit, and let the mixture settle a bit (not totally). The mixture should be fairly cool.
- Gently fold in the whipped cream, place into a glass bowl and cool in the refrigerator Passion fruit is now being admitted into international cuisines… something that should have been done a long, long time ago.

Serves 2

. . . .

Berry punch

This one has alcohol; if you want children to enjoy it add a mix of soda water and lemonade, with orange, passion and pineapple juice. I use strawberries as they are most often available, but you may try, a variety of other berries or fruit.

Ingredients

- 1½ kg strawberries
- 130 gm caster sugar
- 250 ml dry sherry/rum
- 4 x 750 bottles of riesling wine (or sparkling)
- dash angostura bitters (good dash)
- ice

Method

- In a large container, place all the ingredients save the wine and bitters. Let rest for about 6 hours.
- Later when ready, stir in the wine and bitters. Finish off with the crushed ice and enjoy this rather drunken recipe!

Serves 8

· · · · · · · · · · · · · · · · · · · ·

Kenyan fruit punch

You will need a juicer for this recipe, for those who wish for a slightly alcoholic punch add Vodka, a little rum and bitters according to taste. Lots of ice and a few sprigs of mint finish off this potent drink.

Ingredients

- 2 ripe pineapples, remove rind and core, put through the juicer, reserve liquid
- juice of 6 oranges
- juice of 4 limes
- 1 kg fresh passion fruit seeded and one litre boiling water added to this, stir well and let sit for 20 minutes, strain gradually
- 1 kilo sugar, added to the warm passion juice and stirred very well
- 1 punnet strawberries, washed and sliced
- 1 punnet raspberries washed and added. They say never to wash them but what of the *dudus* (insects) hibernating inside?

Method

- Mix all the above, chill, add ice, and serve alongside some soda water and or lemonade.
- The sweetness can be balanced with the soft drinks. Now this is really the real thing.

Serves 4

· · · · · · · · · · · · · · · · · · · ·

Chapter 12

Christmas is here

Christmas ham

'Tis' the season, start early, have everything you need in place, and do not panic.

Ingredients

- 3.5 kg gammon
- water to cover the gammon
- 4 litres apple juice (may be a bit more) or use pineapple juice
- 3 cinnamon sticks
- 4 onions
- 1 tbsp all spice
  Ingredients for the glaze (later):
- 40 cloves to stud
- english mustard to cover gammon
- brown sugar to 'plaster' on.

Method

- Place the gammon in a large pan and cover completely with cold water, bring to a swift boil, drain and rinse the gammon and the pan too.
- Place the gammon in the large pan again and cover with the apple juice completely
- Add the cinnamon sticks, onions and all spice.
- Bring to boil, and then simmer for about 4 hours. If liquid evaporates, replace with hot water … always making sure it is completely covered.
- Remove from pot and let cool. Peel the rind off with a sharp knife. If there is too much fat, trim a little off.
- Pre heat oven to 220°C. Score the ham into a diamond pattern and stud with the cloves decoratively.
- Plaster the English mustard all over then press the brown sugar.
- Place the gammon on a tray and place in the oven.
- Roast for about 30 – 40 minutes or until a golden crust forms. Let rest for 30 minutes before carving. This resting time is great as it gives you time to finish off the preparations for vegetables, gravy, and to 'touch' up the other little details that have to be done at the last minute … make short list to remind yourself.

Serves 8

Traditional roast turkey

I have chosen a simple no fuss recipe that I have used over the years. The Turkey should be completely defrosted and out of the fridge an hour before cooking. Ovens vary a lot so try to get to know yours. The chart below gives approximate times for the bird. The best way to know that it is cooked through is to poke a fork behind the knee joint of the thigh – if the juices are clear it is done. If not, put it back to the oven. Remember to let it rest, cover with foil for at least 45 minutes. Make the gravy at this point plus any other remaining chores. As I indicated before make a list of how best to use this valuable time.

Weight	Time
2.25 kg	1½ hours
3.5 kg	1¾ hours
4.5 kg	2 hours
5.5 kg	2½ hours
6.7 kg	2¾ hours
7.5 kg	3 hours
9 kg	3½ hours

Set the oven temp to 200° C for the first 40 minutes, then turn it down to 180° C (use a timer to remind yourself). The total time used for cooking should be around two hours.

Ingredients

- 4½ kg turkey rinsed and dried using paper towels, inside and out
- 200 gm butter
- salt and freshly milled pepper
- 1 tbsp mixed herbs
- 1 bunch fresh tarragon (chopped)
- 7 onions (quartered)
- 4 lemons (quartered)
- 2 head garlic separated
- 300 gm streaky bacon

Method

- Rub the turkey inside and out with the butter, season inside and out with the salt, freshly milled pepper and herbs, place the onions, lemons and garlic inside the cavity. The extra can be laid besides the bird on the roasting tray.
- Cover the turkey with the bacon, over lapping thickly. Place in the oven, baste every ½ an hour. If it seems to brown too fast, cover the top part with foil loosely. Generally this is not needed, but hey not all ovens are the same.
- Check it is cooked through as I indicated earlier. Cover with foil, let rest for 45 minutes.

- Quickly have a glass of wine to recover and now make the gravy. Remember the leftovers can be used the following day, cold, in salad, or sandwiches. Have a lot of mustard available.

Serves 8

· · · · · · · · · · · · · · · · · · ·

The gravy
Some of this has to be started early and then finished off as the bird rests.

Ingredients

- giblets from the turkey
- a small bunch of fresh mixed herbs tied together (thyme, oregano, parsley, rosemary)
- 1 onion halved
- 1 stick celery
- 8 black peppercorns
- 1 chicken stock cube
- 1 litre water
- 15 gm butter
- 1½ tbsp corn flour
- ½ cup white wine

Method

- In a pan place the giblets, fresh herbs onion, celery, black peppercorns, stock cube and water.
- Bring to boil and then simmer for 2 hours, skimming the froth as it appears.
- Strain. From the turkeys roasting tray, pour as much as the fat as you an off, reserving the valuable juices.
- Place the tin on a low heat to begin with, add the butter and corn flour mix madly and scrape the residue from the tin as well.
- Remove from heat, add the wine and the strained giblet stock, gradually (not all of it yet) stirring all the time.
- Put back on a medium heat and continue to stir. It should thicken. Now if too thick add some more stock, if too thin reduce a bit, it needs to boil for about 2 minutes. Now every chef's nightmare ... if it is lumpy, do not fret, put it through a medium sieve, stir and keep warm. Remember to check and correct the seasoning. Now that was fun, eh?

· · · · · · · · · · · · · · · · · · ·

Creamed spinach

Quite treat, if you like the spinach whole just do not whiz it at the end. Try to squeeze out as much water as possible there will always be some left, but at least it is home made and it is good. Again as it only needs to be heated through once after the whiz you will have time to attend to other vital essentials of this festive meal.

Ingredients

- 2 kg Italian spinach washed
- 50 gm butter
- 2 cloves garlic
- good pinch nutmeg
- salt and freshly milled pepper
- 4 tbsp double cream
  To add later after it has been puréed:
- 1 cup toasted pine nuts or chopped almonds
- 4 tbsp toasted sesame seeds

Method

- In a large pan, over a high flame, have about just under 1 cup of salted water at a rolling boil.
- Add the spinach handful at a time, stirring in between till all of it is done. It needs to cook for a minute.
- Remove, cool a little, and remove extra water by simply squeezing the spinach between your hands. Using the same pan (why wash up more and more pans? Melt the butter, add the garlic, sauté for 30 seconds, add the spinach, nutmeg, season, and the cream and whiz in a food processor.
- Return to pan, heat through when you are ready to eat, place in a warm serving dish, tossing in the nuts and sesame seeds.

Serves 8

....

Mulled wine

Traditionally drunk at Christmas or new year, this rich warming drink sets the tempo for the occasion, makes you slightly tipsy and light hearted ... how wonderful (keep children at bay!). Mix together in a large glass bowl.

Ingredients

- 1 bottle of red wine
- 2 cloves
- 2 cinnamon sticks
- ½ tsp ground ginger (fresh)
- grated zest of 1 orange (organic)
- juice of 2 oranges

- good pinch of nutmeg
- a tbsp of gin
- brown sugar to taste

Method

- Let this mix sit for about 3 hours before required.
- Place in a pan and bring to a brisk boil … remove the second this happens, otherwise all the alcohol will evaporate.
- Serve in dainty coffee cups. Ever, so comforting.

Serves 4–6 … depends on your cups, etc.

. . . .

Roast potatoes

These are really addictive and worth the wait. Pre-heat the oven to 20°C.

Ingredients

- 1½ kg medium sized potatoes, peeled and cut in half
- water
- 1½ tsp salt
- cooking fat or oil

Method

- Place the potatoes in a pan, covered with cold water and the salt. Bring them to a rolling boil for about 10 minutes. Tip the water out and put lid on pan and shake the potatoes about so that they 'roughen' up a bit.
- Melt the cooking fat so as to have about 2½ cm of fat floating, heat this on top of the stove.
- Remove from heat and cautiously tip the potatoes in the fat and coat them well.
- Place in the oven for about 50 minutes or so, turning the potatoes only once.
- They should be golden brown and tender, once again take them out, tip most of the fat out and replace potatoes in the oven for 5 minutes.
- Serve straight away. Ever so yummy!

Serves 8

. . . .

Celebration rice pudding

A slant on the normal style quite exotic and very tropical. If you don't have a double boiler simply use two pans, one larger with simmering water and a smaller one on top with the ingredients.

Ingredients

- 75 gm Rice soaked for an hour in water
- 300 ml water
- 25 gm unsalted water
- 1 l milk
- 2 cinnamon sticks
- 4 tbsp sugar
- 2 tbsp double cream
- 30 gm chopped almonds
- 15 gm raisins or sultanas soaked in warm water for an hour
- raspberries sauce
- 140 gm raspberries
- 3 tbsp icing sugar
- extra raspberries for decoration

Method

- In a pan, simmer the rice with the water for 5 minutes, add the butter and stir until it reduces, then add the milk, cinnamon sticks and sugar, keep stirring for 5 minutes.
- Place the contents to the top part of the double boiler, the bottom pan having simmering water. Let this cook slowly for an hour, stir every now and then, adding more milk if is too thick. Stir in the double cream, almonds and raisins.
- Remove the cinnamon sticks … check the sweetness. You may like to add a little bit more sugar.
- Keep the pudding warm or it can also be served chilled. If you are going to have it chilled, cover directly with cling film on the rice to prevent another skin forming. *Raspberries sauce:*
- Place the raspberries in a pan over a medium heat with the sugar; stir crushing some of the berries.
- Serve alongside the rice pudding, trickling a little over the pudding, as a cute presentation.
- Place whole raspberries around. For that extra zing drizzle a bit of honey over and with a sieve sprinkle the raspberries with a little icing sugar.

Serves 4

. . . .

Happy poached pears

Probably the easiest dessert to make and one of the most delicious. Served with good Italian ice cream, topped with nuts, or simply whipped cream finishes off any meal with a lot of style and flair ... simplicity is the art; believe me.

Ingredients

- 6 cups water
- 4 cups dry red wine
- ½ cup dambuie or cointreau
- 4 cups sugar (less if you like)
- 2 cloves
- 2 sticks cinnamon
- 1 vanilla pod slit in half
- 8 pears with only 1 cm strips peeled off (1 cm left on and 1 cm peeled, etc) leave stem on

Method

- In a pan over a medium heat, add all the ingredients except the pears.
- Stir till sugar is dissolved; add the pears and simmer for 20 minutes or till pears are tender.
- If the liquid gets too syrupy add a little water.
- Serve either hot or cold with ice cream and nuts or whipped cream ... add some icing sugar to the whipped cream.

Serves 8

. . . .

Appendix: Weights and Measures

Dry Measures

Metric	Imperial	Liquid Measures	
15 g	½ oz	30 ml	1 fl oz
30 g	1 oz	60 ml	2 fl oz
60 g	2 oz	100 ml	3 fl oz
90 g	3 oz	125 ml	4 fl oz
125 g	4 oz (lb)	150 ml	5 fl oz(¼ pint)
155 g	5 oz	190 ml	6 fl oz
185 g	6 oz	250 ml	8 fl oz
220 g	7 oz	300 ml	10 fl oz (½ pint)
250 g	8 oz (½ lb)	500 ml	16 fl oz
280 g	9 oz	600 ml	20fl oz (1 pint)
315 g	10 oz		
345 g	11 oz (¾ lb)		
375 g	12 oz		
410 g	13 oz		
500 g	16 oz (1 lb)		
1 kg	32 oz (2.2 lb)		

Abbreviations

gas	–	medium heat electricity	Med. heat	–	medium flame
fl oz	–	fluid	Ml	–	millilitre
gm	–	gram	Oz	–	ounce
High heat	–	high flame	tbsp	–	tablespoon
kg	–	kilogram	tsp	–	teaspoon
Low heat	–	low flame			

Oven temperature (approximate)

	° Celsius	0 Fahrenheit	Gas mark
Very slow	120	250	1
Slow	150	300	2
Mod. slow	160	325	3
Moderate	180	350	4 – 5
Hot	200	400	6
Very hot	230	450	7

The recipes indicate the number of people who can be served, e.g. Serves 2, 4, etc. The quantities of the ingredients can be doubled or halved to cater for double or half the servings respectively. Do not combine metric and imperial measures. Stick to the measures you start with. All vegetables and meats should be of the best quality. This always reflects upon your final result. Measurements in tablespoons, teaspoons and cups are level.

Glossary

Aioli garlic mayonnaise – the crushed garlic is added to the egg yolk before the oil is added slowly (see under "mayonnaise").

Alcohol – wine, brandy, cognac, beer and even gin are commonly used for cooking. Alcohol gives a distinctive taste when used in cooking. If you are against it, try non-alcoholic beer or wine. Obviously the spirits cannot be substituted. Normally in cooking the alcohol is reduced by boiling, but a little more can be added before heating and serving.

Aubergine – egg plant, a deep purple egg-shaped vegetable. Sometimes quite bitter. To remove the bitterness, slice and sprinkle with salt, leave for 20 minutes and rinse in cold water.

Avocado – once cut or pureed, should be mixed with lime to prevent discolouration. Leaving the stone in also helps.

Adjustment – some recipes can be changed to suit individual taste for example quantities of stock, garlic, ginger, wine and cream. The same goes for thickening agents such as tomato puree, corn flour, etc.

Bain-marie see double boiler
(Author: note these look like recipes. Can we include in the main text)

Beef stock
To make:
Ingredients
- 2 kg (2.2 lb) bones from beef
- 3 onions
- 2 celery sticks
- 3 carrots
- 3 bay leaves
- 2 tsp black pepper corns
- 5 l water (20 cups)
- 3 l water (12 cups) extra

Method
- Brown the bones with the onions in a moderate oven for 1 hour.
- Transfer to a pan with the rest of the ingredients and simmer for 3 hours. Add more water if needed.
- Skim every hour. Strain. Reduce.

Black pepper – always use freshly ground or milled pepper as the flavour is really different from the powdered variety.

Blanche – to plunge food in boiling water for a minute or so. Sometimes used to help get rid of the bitter taste and to improve the food quality when frozen.

Bouquet Garni – consists of parsley stalks, thyme and a bay leaf tied together. Always be careful not to overuse herbs.

Breadcrumbs – can be made by grating 2 to 3-day-old bread. Alternatively, put fresh sliced bread in the oven or in a toaster for a while and crush.

Brine – a solution of salt and water.

Butter – a good medium for cooking, but beware as it burns quickly, especially over a high flame. In hot sauces that use butter at the end of cooking, add a little bit more than stated in the ingredients. It improves texture and looks great. If possible, use unsalted butter.

Cardamom – adds aromatic value to food. Use sparingly.

Cheese – when grated and refrigerated, it keeps longer. Older blocks can be substituted for parmesan cheese.

Chillies – available in both fresh and dried form. Use with care and wash hands after handling.

Coriander (fresh) – also known as dhania, cilantro or Chinese parsley. It is easily grown and is available at green grocers. It has a distinctive taste and is often wrongly substituted with parsley by some authors. Keep wrapped in grease-proof paper in the refrigerator. There is no substitute.

Coriander seeds – these have a totally different taste from fresh coriander. Roast them lightly and grind in a coffee mill. Keep in a closed bottle.

Corn flour (corn starch) – used as a thickening agent, in this collection as a substitute to plain flour as it is not as heavy. In some recipes cream is used to prevent splitting.

Courgette (zucchini, squash) – a member of the marrow family. A delicious vegetable which needs little cooking. For salads, just blanch.

Couscous – cracked wheat or semolina grains used extensively in the Middle East. Normally it is steamed or boiled with a little butter. Variations for cooking depend upon the manufacturer. It is advisable to follow their instructions.

Crab – if intended for use in a cold salad, it should be boiled for about 20 minutes. If it is to be used in a hot dish which requires further cooking, boil for about 15 minutes.

Cream – its usefulness in cooking cannot be overemphasised. Always use fresh cream, and once added to food, do not boil as this makes it curdle. In all the recipes using cream I have indicated the use of corn flour as a precaution.

Cumin seeds – roast lightly and grind. Keep in a closed bottle.

Dhania *see* Coriander

Dhana jira – a mixed spice made of coriander and cumin seeds, roasted and crushed together in a coffee grinder. Proportions: 4 tbsp cumin seeds and 2 tbsp coriander seeds. Keep in a closed glass jar.

Double boiler – the same as a bain-marie. If you do not have one, do not despair. Use a large pan, add hot water to it, place it on the stove at medium heat and place another pan in it. The water should not boil.

Eggs – buy these when you need them. Usually, those from free-range chickens are best. After boiling eggs, plunge in cold water for 15 seconds. This prevents the yolks from darkening and makes them easier to peel. Scrambled eggs are best prepared with a little milk and butter over a double boiler. This may sound tedious, but it's worth the trouble. Add a little cream when the eggs are nearly done. Pre-cooked asparagus, mushrooms or shrimps can also be added.

Fat or oil – extra fat left floating in a dish should be skimmed off.

Flaming – to add brandy/cognac at the end of cooking and ignite. This enhances the flavour of the dish.

Garlic butter – used in cooking or crowning steaks by mixing butter with crushed garlic (according to your taste) and parsley and freezing it in a roll of foil. It is ready to use whenever you need it.

Garlic and ginger – potent but tasty flavourings. As they are often-used ingredients, both can be peeled and ground to a paste in large quantities (separately) for handy use. Mix with a little salt and olive or corn oil and keep in the refrigerator for 2 weeks. They can also be frozen in batches. This way, they can keep for up to 2 months without losing their flavour. Avoid the powdered form.

Garam masala – often mistaken for curry powder, although it is very different. Basic mix:

Ingredients
- 1 cup cumin seeds
- ½ cup coriander seeds
- 1 tbsp black peppercorns
- ½ tbsp cinnamon
- ½ tbsp cardamom
- ½ tsp nutmeg

Method
- Roast under grill for 2 – 3 minutes until you can smell the spices. Cool.
- Grind finely in a mill used for spices only. This way you can also grind your own cumin seeds to make cumin powder, coriander seeds to make coriander powder and so on. Freshly milled spices are much nicer.

Green peppers – sweet peppers – not to be confused with the hot version.

Harissa – a hot paste made with red chilli, pepper, salt, olive oil and garlic (optional). Can be easily made at home with the above ingredients, to suit your taste. Beware of those chillies. Keep refrigerated. Do not make vast quantities as it "bubbles" after a few weeks.

Herbs – use fresh herbs where possible. Most of the recipes in this book indicate the use of dried herbs, so if you can find the fresh version, remember to use slightly more than the recipe indicates.

Horseradish – can be bought bottled or if you have it fresh, peel and grate and mix with mayonnaise or whipped cream. Season with salt, pepper and mustard.

Hollandaise sauce

Ingredients
- 2 egg yolks, beaten
- 125 gm (4 oz) butter, melted
- 4 tbsp dry white wine
- 2 tsp lime juice
- salt and pepper

Warning: Never heat this sauce violently as it will curdle.
- Heat the wine in a pan until it reduces by half. Keep aside, place the egg yolk in a bain-marie or double boiler and whisk energetically.
- Add the wine gradually. Still stirring fast, add the butter very slowly. The sauce will start to take form.
- Remove from the heat and add the lime juice and seasoning. If the sauce curdles, add a little hot water drop by drop, stirring constantly.

Serving suggestion: pour over chicken breasts, garnish with parsley and serve immediately.

Lassi – a wonderful cool drink made with yoghurt, water, salt, pepper and cumin, whisked together. If you like it sweet, add a little honey or sugar.

Lettuce – there are many interesting varieties available. Experiment with them all: curly endive, coral, cos, iceberg, red oak, green oak, etc. Always wash well.

Lime or lemon – I have indicated the use of lime juice because it has a better taste. Lemons sometimes tend to be sour and bitter. You can use either.

Lobster – if possible, buy live lobsters. To kill (dress) them, plunge into boiling water for about 3 minutes (if it is going to be cooked again in another dish). If not, they should be boiled for at least 20 minutes. Alternatively, freeze them alive and cook when required. There is quite a debate among culinary buffs about which method is better. If you can't face being your own butcher, buy dressed lobster. For home use, it is just as good.

Mayonnaise – ingredients should be at room temperature. Often, mayonnaise is found to be too "eggy"; this is because too much egg yolk is used and not enough oil. To make:

Ingredients
- 2 egg yolks (for aioli, add 2 – 3 cloves of garlic, crushed)
- 1 tsp whole grain mustard
- 1 tbsp wine vinegar
- 275 ml (½ pint) equal mix of olive and salad oil
- salt and pepper
- 2 tbsp hot water

Method
- Place mustard with the egg yolks in a liquidizer and put at speed 2 or 3. Add salt, pepper and vinegar.

- Start putting in the oil, drop by drop. Increase the speed of the liquidizer a little and continue adding the oil slowly. Once the oil is being absorbed fast, you can gradually increase the speed with which you are dropping it in. When all the oil has been incorporated, correct the seasoning to suit your taste.
- Finally, add the hot water. Refrigerate. The process of oil addition is a delicate skill. You may not get the hang of it until you have tried it out a few times, but be patient.
- After a while, you will know exactly when to increase the oil flow.

Mustard – you can make your own mustard at home and flavour it with garlic, black pepper or tarragon. Buy whole mustard seeds from Indian ration shops. A fine sieve will get rid of the tiny stones, but you will still have to pick through to get rid of the larger ones. Start off with a small quantity. To make:

Ingredients
- 250 gm (8 oz) whole mustard seeds
- 500 ml wine vinegar or malt vinegar
- 1 cup white wine
- a little oil
- salt and pepper

Method
- Mildly roast the mustard seeds under a grill. Cool.
- Place half the seeds in a liquidizer with enough vinegar and wine to cover. Liquidize to the required consistency.
- Repeat the process with the remaining mustard seeds.
- Season and flavour as you like. Refrigerate. The flavour improves with time. However, do not make too much as it does not keep for long.

Olive oil – use extra virgin which is the best. Some people cannot digest pure olive oil; which is the reason why the use of ½ olive oil and ½ corn (salad) oil is indicated in this collection. But if you have no such problem, use it pure.

Parsley – blanch quickly and freeze for emergency use.

Pasta – cook according to manufacturers' instructions, adding a little oil when boiling. If you must re-heat pasta in an emergency, stand it in a large colander and pour 2 kettlefuls of boiling water over it and then add some butter or oil. Most people like their pasta *al dente*, which means tender but firm to the tooth.

Poach – to simmer with wine, herbs, carrots, onions and a bay leaf.

Potato sauté – peel potatoes and cube evenly. Plunge into salted boiling water for 4 minutes or until boiling resumes. Melt some butter and oil in a pan (enough to cover the potatoes) over a medium fire and gradually put in the potatoes when the fat is hot. In this instance you must use butter and oil.

Pressure cooker – a great way to save time. If you are familiar with one, you can shorten the time required for long recipes, but most of the recipes in this collection do not require the use of a pressure cooker. A friend of mine used one for the first time;

though what she did I will never know. The lid was in her hand and the chicken bits were stuck on the ceiling. Luckily she was not hurt, but I'm sure she will not be amused by my telling you this. Horror stories aside, however, if used as per instructions, they are perfectly safe.

Reduce – to boil a sauce or liquid to the desired consistency. Place a pan on high heat for a minute or two and add the liquid. The evaporation reduces the sauce. This is done when a sauce is too thin for the dish. Alcohol is usually reduced to about ½ its original amount. Sometimes just a little is added again at the end of cooking.

Salsify – boil it for about 45 minutes with a little vinegar and then peel. It should be left in a bowl of cold water with vinegar prior to use. Served as a gratin or with lemon, butter and parsley, it is an unusual vegetable delight.

Saffron – used for its distinctive flavour and as a natural food colouring. A pinch dissolved in a ¼ cup of hot water goes a long way in rice, pasta dishes.

Salad oil *see* corn oil

Sauté – to fry in a small quantity of oil over high heat, for a short while.

Seal – to fry on very high heat for a short time. This stops the meat juices from flowing out.

Snow-peas (mange-tout) – cut the top and tail and either blanch or stir-fry. Little cooking is needed and they should be crisp.

Soya sauce – a salty, dark brown substance made from fermented soya beans.

Stock cubes – handy when home-made stock is not available. However, they tend to be very salty so be careful when adding salt to a dish where you have used stock cubes. To create your own, portion home-made stock and freeze in little plastic bags or in an ice tray.

Soups – for the packet or tinned variety, add fresh vegetables or meat (asparagus, peas, onions, cooked chicken, etc). You can also add garlic, milk or cream and freshly ground black pepper to hide that "packet" taste.

Tabasco – trade name of a famous piquant sauce. You can use a little cayenne pepper, if it is unavailable, although it is not as good.

Tamarind – the pulpy fruit from a tree of the same name. It is available in some supermarkets and Indian ration shops. Buy ½ kg and soak in hot water with 6 dates, soaked and chopped up finely. Allow it to cool, then strain and add more water, if needed. Mix with salt, chilli, sugar, fresh coriander, grated carrots and a teaspoonful of roasted, crushed cumin. A wonderful sauce to go with curry or barbecued meat.

Turmeric – when whole, it is a hard, yellow substance. In powder form, it is still yellow, burns easily whilst cooking and gives a musky taste. It is also an antiseptic, hence its use in curry and some medicines.

Tomatoes – to skin, let them stand in boiling water for about 2 – 3 minutes and allow to cool. The skin should come off easily. The "stubborn" ones may need a little more time in the hot water. Some people discard the pips, but it does not make a significant difference.

Tarragon – the flavour of the French variety is better than the Russian, which is more widely available. To preserve, place in a clean glass jar with white wine vinegar. Keep refrigerated.

Vinaigrette –
To make:
Ingredients
- 75 ml wine vinegar
- 175 ml olive oil or mix ½ that amount with any other salad oil
- salt and pepper
- mustard to taste
- 2 cloves garlic, crushed
- herbs of your choice

Method

Mix all these ingredients together and serve with cold salad.

Vinegar – try to find wine vinegar or malt vinegar. Avoid the white variety which contains acetic acid alone.

Vegetables – always wash well, especially for cold salads as these are often the culprits in cases of stomach upsets.

Wines – for cooking, there is no need to buy extravagantly expensive wine. It usually needs to be reduced. A little more may be added at the end of cooking, but remember to heat it through for a minute.

Worcestershire sauce – made with tamarind, malt vinegar, molasses, spices and anchovies. It is available in shops under various trade names.

White sauce
To make:
Ingredients
- 20 gm butter
- 20 gm com flour
- 285 ml milk
- 2 tbsp cream
- 1 onion with 4 cloves stuck into it
- salt and pepper

Method
- Put the butter and flour into a heavy pan over medium fire.
- Cook until it bubbles, but do not allow it to brown.
- Remove from the fire and gradually add the milk, stirring constantly. Return to the heat until the sauce thickens.
- Add the onion and let the sauce simmer gently for 5 minutes. Add a little more milk if too thick. Season with salt and pepper.
- To enhance the taste, you can also add cream and a 1 tsp of butter. Makes 200 ml (approximately 7 fl oz).

Index

Printed in the United States
By Bookmasters